1984

"I want out of this marriage". Although it was July the rain was thumping down and the two lorries on either side of the car seemed to be collaborating on a meat sandwich with the inhabitants of the Christie Ford Escort providing the protein.

"Will you shut up or I am going to crash the car!" "The way I am feeling I do not care if you crash the car. What I am saying is that it is over and I want out. This holiday has been the final straw."

No wonder there are lakes in the Lake District with all the rain they get. The artics on either side were struggling to cope with the Shap gradient. A space opened out in front of me and I put the foot down and pulled in to the safety of the inside lane.

I looked over to the front passenger seat and our twelve year old son, Max, was sitting with his head bowed and tears streaming down his cheeks. I could feel my temper rising.

"OK. I agree that it is over but we cannot talk about this in a car with Max listening. I'll go to a lawyer when we get home but you have got to keep quiet because I am having enough trouble coping with this weather and the lorries".

"Alright I'll say no more but you must do something about it when we get home".

"OK, OK. But for the time being give me some peace".

There was silence.

That's the way I remember the day on which Margaret and I finally agreed that our 19-year-old marriage was at an end.

1937

This was the year my parents, Bridget and Peter, came over to Scotland from Ireland. They were brought up in Arigna, a place of mountains and lakes on the border of counties Roscommon and Leitrim. Arigna is the only place in Ireland to have coalmines and traditionally the miners of Arigna came over to Scotland to work in the coalfields. Many of them settled in the Lothians and, when my father crossed the Irish Sea at age 26, he lived with relatives in West Lothian and found work in the building trade. This was not the first time he has made the crossing because he was actually born in South Lanarkshire in the little village of Tarbrax. His father Pat had come over from Arigna to work, met a Scottish girl, married her, and had five children - my dad was born in 1911. Times were hard and as a wee boy my father Peter and his younger brother Pat were taken to Arigna and left there to be brought up by their grandparents. So by birth I am three quarters Irish and one quarter Scottish. Many years ago I had cause to look at my father's birth certificate and was amazed to see that he had been registered as "Peter Christy". I asked him why he had not stuck with the Irish spelling and he told me that he got fed up correcting people and just decided to go with "Christie". I thought of changing back to the original name - but again it was just too much bother. My dad had left school at 12 and never really fancied it. Writing was not his strong point but he was sharp and worldly wise and was blessed with a good nature and sense of humour that made him the best of companions. He was a wonderful caring and loving father. He had worked underground in the mines in Arigna but, being slightly claustrophobic, decided it was not for him. He was fairly tall and tremendously strong and, like many Irishmen before him, he could use a shovel to good effect. Before too long the fact that there was something going on behind his eyes was recognised by his bosses and he was promoted to be a crane driver.

In 1937 Bridget was 22 years old. She had loved school and had stayed on until she was 14 helping the teachers with the younger ones. Her dream was to be a school teacher but family economics meant that it was a dream that could never be realised; she was needed to work on the croft at home and, until she left to follow Peter to Scotland, that is what she did. She used to say that she could never eat chicken because she had wrung the necks of so many. However, the cover of a little sauce was usually enough for her to "make an exception this once".

She arrived in Scotland a few months after Peter and immediately found work as a downstairs maid in Gullane, 18 miles east of Edinburgh. When interviewing Bridget for the job, the lady of the house warned her that the cook was extremely cantankerous and a bit of a martinet. Downstairs maids tended not to last long. Bridget made up her mind to give the cook no cause for complaint and decided that she was always going to be pleasant and friendly towards her and ignore any lack of kindness towards herself. Before too long the pair of them were bosom pals and the cook could not do enough for the "wee lassie". She even took Bridget to see the 1938 Empire Exhibition in Glasgow.

Although living in Scotland, in those days Bridget and Peter considered themselves to be Irish and thought those who had fought for independence to be heroes. Bridget was teased mercilessly by my sons and me when, in later life, she let it slip that at 14 she had been secretary of the local branch of the IRA and that she really enjoyed wearing the wee beret and skirt that went with the job. As the years went on my parents became integrated into the Scottish way of life and brought my brother and I up to be fiercely proud of being Scottish. However in 1937 their allegiance was to Eire, which had just been created from the Irish Free State.

War was looming and the talk was of all able-bodied men being called up into the military. Peter, who was not usually someone to run away from a fight, had no inclination to fight in a war in which Eire was not involved and decided that he was off back home to Arigna leaving Wee Bridget alone in the big house in Gullane. She was fully behind this decision and had actually persuaded him to make the return trip.

He was only there a few weeks when Prime Minister, Neville Chamberlain, returned from Munich after his meeting with Hitler and announced that the threat of war was over and there was to be "peace in our time". And so it was back on the boat and back to Scotland and his darling Bridget.

In 1939 they were married in St Mary's Cathedral in Edinburgh and eventually settled in a top story single-end in Nicolson Street directly opposite what used to be the Empire and is now the Festival Theatre.

When war broke out Peter was working in the Marine Gardens in Portobello on the type of job which was considered a priority for the war effort and which gave him exemption from National Service. Bridget found work in one of the grand houses in Edinburgh's Morningside district.

In October 1943 they left Nicolson Street and moved to a "Corporation" flat in the Loganlea district of Edinburgh between Leith and Portobello. For the first 22 years of her life Bridget had lived in a tiny cottage that had no electricity and no running water or toilet. Paraffin lamps and candles provided the light, peat from the hillside the heat and if you wanted water there was the stream that ran down the hill past the side of the cottage. If you needed the toilet you just picked your spot on the hill and could admire the view over Lough Allan as you did your business. She now had a two bedroom flat with electricity, running water and, would you believe, an inside toilet. There was even a bath. She was the happiest colleen in Scotland.

Both my parents were good natured and great company but they both had an Irish temper. They took a bit of arousing but when they let go you did not want to mess with them. In this respect I am a clone of my parents. Joyce Souness, a teaching colleague (star), once confided to me that she had brought a friend along to a prize giving and that her friend had commented what a nice guy I seemed to be. With relish Joyce related to me that she had put her right, "He's not, he's a wee bastard".

On the first day of September 1940 their first son was born in Elsie Inglis Maternity Hospital, exactly one year after the outbreak of war. Little Peter was born with a foot that was not properly formed and spent the first couple of years of his young life in and out of hospital having operations so that he could walk properly and live a normal life.

I came into the world on 16th December 1942. My earliest memory of my big brother was of him as a four year old collecting stones and going to the bottom of our tenement with a pile at his feet and then throwing stones at the local bairns as they passed on their way to Craigentinny Primary School. "Craigie" was of course a Proddie school but I do not think that his stone throwing was in any way motivated by religious prejudice – he just liked throwing stones at people.

Maybe I should start by telling you his good points and there were lots of those. He had, throughout his life, a loving nature and would never do any thing really bad. He did not count stealing by the way as being in any way bad. If he liked you he would do anything for you and go to lots of trouble to help you. He was bright with a wicked sense of humour and could be great company but only for a short time – usually round about an hour was as long as he could go before he became irritated by the company and started to be fractious.

One thing I did marvel at was the way in which he was able to amuse himself. There were no toys or television in the 1940's and you had to find ways of keeping yourself occupied. He had no problem doing this. In the good weather he would be outside in the back green with a jam-jar catching bees or trying to catch pigeons by "cooing" at them. For bad weather days he invented his own complicated game. He would pull out the ends of the "big table" to extend it and then cover it with scraps of paper which he had carefully cut out. Each scrap represented a soldier and on that table he would play for hours fighting imaginary battles. I never really got the hang of what he was up to but nobody was allowed near the table whilst the war was being waged.

 The thing he liked doing best however was stealing. I cannot remember a time when he was not stealing. When I was three or four he used to take me into the local shops and coach me how to distract the shopkeeper so that he could steal some sweets or place a comic up his jumper.

 When he was eight the film of the Dickens' novel "Oliver Twist" came out with Alec Guinness playing the part of Fagan who, you will recollect, had a band of children stealing for him. Fagan was supposed to be a villain but to Peter he was a hero. One of the best scenes in David Lean's wonderful film was when Fagan was teaching the youngsters to pick pockets. We used to play that scene at home countless times as Peter strived to improve his skills as a pickpocket. It was my pocket that got picked. You can become good at almost anything if the motivation is there and I am proud to relate that my brother was the best pickpocket I have ever met – not that I know many pickpockets.

 Having Peter as a brother taught me many things and next to my mother he was the biggest influence in forming the character that was to take me through life. I never doubted his love for me but he made my young life hell. When not at school we were alone for most of the time because Dad was usually working away from home and Bridget was out at one of her many cleaning jobs. Peter had bullying to a fine art. If I did not concede to his every whim I was punched - never too hard, but just enough to make me miserable.

 This went on until I was about 14 and growing strong with all the football I was playing. I decided I had had enough of being bullied and was going to do something about it.

 It was about five o'clock in the afternoon and Peter had just come in from his work; he was an apprentice television and radio mechanic. He ordered me to run to the shop and get him five fags.

"Go yourself", I shouted at him in anger. He then started to push me.

"Listen, I have had enough of this and it is going to stop"

I then picked up my heavy school shoes and started to put them on.

"That's good. So you are going then", he said.

"No", I answered. "I am putting my shoes on because I am going to kick fuck out of you."

I must have been really angry for, in those days, being an altar boy, I never swore. I could understand his fear because the shoes had just returned from the cobblers having had heavy metal tacks put on the soles and were most definitely fearsome weapons at the end of my strong wee legs.

I then kicked him as hard as I could on the thigh. He screamed, "You're off your fucking head" and opened the front door and, before slamming it behind him, shouted "I'll go for my ain fags."

From that moment he never again hit me. Anytime he started to become aggressive I would pick up my shoes and he would say, "OK, we're not going through that again".

Spending my childhood with Peter made me tougher than I would have been without him and also taught me how to put up with adversity and not allow it to get you down. Being bullied every day was a good preparation for the difficulties that life presents and the day of the school shoes going on has been repeated in a metaphorical sense many times.

Don't get the idea that I was a poor picked upon wee soul because that was not the case – but I was deformed. Perhaps I should have told you what Peter and I looked like. Well both of us were small. Fully grown I am 5 feet 7 inches (nearly) and he is a good inch smaller. His looks come from our dad's side of the family and mine from my mother's. He was dark and sharp featured and I am fairer and not sharp featured but with a huge head. As long as I can remember I was called "Big Heid" by all the boys in Loganlea Drive. One of the older ones used to take great pleasure in putting his hands round my head and loudly stating "I would'nae mind having a heid like that full of threepenny bits". Peter knew how much I hated being called Big Heid and so whenever I failed to do his bidding the nickname was used liberally.

I thought it could not get any worse and then it did. The popular comics were the "Beano" and the "Dandy" which were both essential reading for all Scottish children in the years after the war. In one of them (I don't remember which) a new character called Peam was introduced. Peam could do wonderful things with the box of magic pills he always carried. Nothing wrong with that, but the cartoonist had drawn him as a tiny boy with an absolutely massive head. I was no longer Big Heid but was now Peam, which I hated just as much. It stayed with me until my mid-twenties and I would cringe when people used it although by that time they were not aware that it had any connection to my deformity.

Am I really deformed? Eventually, as I grew, the "heid" became less out of proportion to the rest of my body and remarks about its size reduced in frequency. But the fact is that I do have an unusually large cranium. I have never found a hat that even nearly fitted. Not even the adjustable sun-shades favoured by golfers are big enough even when at maximum size. So I am not really deformed, but as a child I thought I was and the comments passed about the size of my head were a constant source of unhappiness.

However, in common with brother Peter, I am not short in the ego department and when I look back on my early childhood I have to admit to getting involved in rather a large number of fights. From age three to age five I attended the local nursery at Craigentinny Primary School and then, in 1948, went on to the Catholic St Ninian's Primary School. I enrolled at St Ninian's with a bit of a reputation having been the "bully" of the nursery. Being the "bully" did not mean that you were a real bully but that you were the best fighter in the establishment. I cannot remember having had any real fights at nursery but can recollect that I was more than a little bit proud of the title "bully".

My first day at St Ninian's is one I will never forget. Everything went as normal until the morning interval. Peter was proud of having a wee brother with a formidable reputation as a fighter and was determined that I was going to make my mark early at the new school. At morning interval he got hold of me and we did a tour of the playground.

"My wee brother can do you" he would state to the unprepared victim who was older than me and much taller.

"No he cannae", was the normal reply.

"On you go Terence" (My mother insisted on Terence and I became "Terry" only at about age 16 when I started to play juvenile football.)

I would then swing the massive "heid" and give the Edinburgh equivalent of the "Glasgow Kiss". The poor victim was left in tears clutching his face.

This scene was repeated another eight or nine times and by the end of the interval my reputation was established. In my first two years at school I had a lot of fights. None of them lasted any length of time. A swing of the "heid" and it was over. When about seven or eight I fought a boy called Andrew Devine who was in the class above me and was a really tough lad. After quite a battle we shook hands and agreed to call it a draw. I realised that it was a better result for me than him and decided that my fighting days were over. Other than my jousts with Peter that was the last fight of my life, although my reputation as being a tough guy stayed with me for many years and even followed me when I went to secondary school.

One bout in my fighting career stands out more than others. Wee Bridget had a number of cleaning jobs. One of these was at Morningside - every Wednesday morning she washed the stairs of the posh flats in

Falcon Avenue. During the school holidays she would take me with her whilst a neighbour looked after Peter whose penchant for taking anything not nailed down meant that it was not a good idea that he should be anywhere near affluent Morningside.

Bridget was washing the stairs and I was playing with some of the local children. One of them made a comment about my mother's weight (for a short time she allowed herself to get really fat). This comment triggered "the heid" into operation with the inevitable result. That was the last time I accompanied my mother to Morningside.

I did try hard to be a good boy and for the first 25 years of my life was a practising Catholic. Bridget was a devout Catholic but my dad worked six days of the week and saw Sunday as the day for a long lie and then a few pints at the Hibs Supporters' Club. As we grew up it became accepted in the family that Peter was his father's boy and I my mother's and so Peter was allowed to miss mass and stay home with dad whilst Bridget and I went to church. If truth be told she was quite happy with this arrangement as it meant she did not have to try and stop Peter stealing the money out of the collection plate. He had perfected the art of appearing to put money into the plate when in fact he was removing it.

I became an altar boy and I loved it. The priests at St Ninian's were Irish and all acted as if they had a hot line to God, but they were good kind men and I have only fond memories of them. The mass was conducted in Latin and that added a great mystique to it for none of us had much idea what the words meant. The only parts which were not in Latin were when the priest turned to the congregation and said the Greek words, "Kyrie elieson" and "Christi elieson" which mean respectively "Lord, have mercy" and "Christ, have mercy". Peter used to say that the reason he stopped attending mass was that one Sunday he arrived late and that the priest embarrassed him by turning to the congregation and announcing, "Christie he lies in."

The priests and the school united to indoctrinate the children into the Catholic Church. Every day started with prayers and the catechism that presented the teaching of the church as fact. There were no shades of grey; Adam and Eve did live in the Garden of Eden and there was a place called Limbo where babies who died before baptism went for all eternity because they had not been cleansed of original sin. Purgatory was where your soul was tidied up after death so that you could enter the kingdom of heaven.

Once a month our teacher marched the class up Marionville Road to the church for confession. Recounting your sins with your pals sitting outside the confessional was stressful, particularly if your confession was heard by Father Higgins. Unlike the other priests he was Scottish and less good natured and forgiving than his Irish colleagues. When I was about eight my mother had beaten me at cards and, being a bad loser, I had thrown the pack of cards at her. I was terribly ashamed of what I had done. How could I treat my darling mother in such a way?

"Bless me father for I have sinned. It is four weeks since my last confession.

"Please father, I got angry with my mother and threw a pack of cards at her."

"Did they hit her?"

"Yes father – they glanced off her head"

I then heard a chair being pushed aside and the door of the priest's side of the confessional opening. The door to the part I was kneeling in was then pulled open and staring down at me was this grey haired giant whose face was red with anger. "Get out of there," he shouted as he grabbed me by the scruff of the neck and lifted me up and propelled me out of the confessional. The 29 other children were staring at me, glad it was not them.

He then whispered to me, "Get down to the front of the church and say 10 "Hail Marys" for your penance and make sure you never do anything like that again."

I made my way to the front sobbing quietly, totally miserable and feeling sorry for myself. On the way back to school my classmates were desperate to know what heinous crime I had committed but I was too ashamed to tell them the truth and told them that I had been caught stealing with Peter.

It never entered my mind to question anything I was told with regard to religion although I did worry about the wee babies stuck in Limbo for all eternity and how my dad could be such a good man when he never went to mass or confession and was going about with a soul blackened with a large number of mortal sins.

Sin had a high profile and I spent a lot of time worrying about the state of my soul and what would happen to me if I was knocked down by a bus. How long was I going to have to spend in the fires of Purgatory? It was also a cause for concern that all impure thoughts were classified as mortal rather than venial sins – and I did have my share of impure thoughts.

On the positive side I had my own guardian angel looking after me and every day with the rest of the class I would pray: "Oh, my good angel, whom God has appointed to be my guardian, enlighten and protect me, direct and govern me during this day. Amen."

We prayed a lot without understanding totally the words of the prayers. "The fruit of thy womb Jesus" is part of the "Hail Mary" but it was not until I was well into my secondary school education that I realised the true meaning of the word "womb". Prior to that I thought that it was some sort of old English word meaning "who art". Come to think of it there was also not a lot of time spent explaining what the "virgin" part of "Virgin Mary" meant.

At age eleven I became an altar boy and loved the job. I was fascinated by the Latin of the mass, the smell of incense, the ringing of the bells during the mass, the candles and just about everything to do with the church. But I had no hankering to be a priest. Our parish priest, Canon Harold, would take me out of the classroom on fairly regular occasions and ask me if I had ever thought of becoming a priest. Frightened to upset someone so distinguished I always said that I would think about it. Truth was I already had an eye for the girls and the idea of a chaste life did not appeal; moreover, Wee Bridget had told me I was to be a teacher.

As a child however none of this bothered me and I loved my school. The teachers cared deeply about the welfare of the children who treated them with great respect. No pupil would ever have dreamt of answering back or questioning the teacher in any way. The headmaster was Mr Quigley who died when I was in my second last year and was replaced by Mr Caden. All of us were in awe of the headmaster and stood to attention whenever he entered our classroom.

At the end of primary school we sat the qualifying exam ("The Qually") to see whether we went to a senior secondary school (Holy Cross) or to a junior secondary (St Anthony's). Of my class of about 30 kids a half dozen or so of us went on to Holy Cross. Some of the girls went to the all girl school St Thomas's and the others to "Tony's". Modesty does not prevent my telling you that I was the brightest in my class and every year gained the prize for "dux of the class". My mother had a relative who became a schoolteacher and it was her ambition that I was going to follow in the footsteps of "Master McCrann". Often I would hear how she could have been a teacher but had to leave school at 14 to help on the croft back in Arigna. She was determined that her bright wee boy was going to be a teacher and get the chances she never had and she drove me hard to do well at school. She was pushing at an open door because I have always loved learning and even today my greatest pleasure is finding out about things. I am never away from "Google" and am seen as a "know-all" by all my mates. I don't mind - rather be a "know-all" than a "know-fuck-all". My dad had no lofty ambitions for my brother or me. All his life he had to work outdoors on building sites in all kinds of weather and his one hope for his sons was that they should get an indoor job.

Besides learning, the other thing I loved at school was football. In a council scheme in the immediate post-war years all the boys played football. We had no television or computer games and so you had to amuse yourself. One of the main ways of doing this was to play football and I played non-stop from about the age of four. Finding a ball to play with was difficult because nobody could afford to buy a proper football. Normally we played with old tennis balls that, for some reason, seemed to be in plentiful supply although nobody played tennis. Finding somewhere to play was easy – there were no motor cars about and so we played in the street with our jackets down as goals. For a proper game we went along to Craigentinny Primary School and played in the playground. There were no grass areas near at hand and normally my legs were covered in scrapes from falling on the hard surfaces.

Our school team was run by John McGrogan who had once played for Hearts (according to legend). "Wee Joe" was a great man and I admired and respected him. He was a great influence in making me the kind of teacher I became. He was a hugely talented pianist and played the organ in St Mary's Cathedral. However his first love was football. I remember Wee Joe coming into our classroom and telling Miss Lamont that King George VI had died. He then turned to our class and said that, if a protestant could be a saint, then King George would be one. I also remember him telling us during one summer that, if we went up town, we would see lots of men dressed like priests. These men, he explained, were not proper priests but were ministers of the Church of Scotland, which was having its General Assembly in Edinburgh. He said you could tell that they were not priests because of their long glum faces. On the last day of the school year in 1954, when I was eleven, he sent for me. When I went into his classroom he presented me with a brand new leather football and told me that I was to practise with it during the long summer holidays. It was unheard of for anybody to have a full sized football or "fully" as we called it and I not only played with it every day but slept with it at night.

When I was eight and Peter ten he got into the school team; he was a clever wee inside forward. The team used to practise after school at St John's playing fields in

Portobello, a bus ride away. I used to tag along with my big brother and go to the practices even though I had no football boots. For those with aspirations of being selected for the team, Friday morning playtime was an exciting time because Wee Joe would pin the team for Saturday's game on the big tree in the middle of the playground.

One Friday in October Peter was off school not well and when I went out into the playground at morning interval I looked at the tree and was overjoyed to find that I had been picked to replace him in the team. At lunchtime I ran home to tell my mother. On hearing the news Peter jumped out of his sick bed and started to thump me. Once my mother had pulled him off me she then faced up to the problem that I did not have football boots and we had no money to buy me a pair. I went back to school with her reassuring me that she would see what she could do. My dad was working away from home and so it was up to Wee Bridget to solve the problem.

And solve it she did. On Friday nights the "Provy Cheque" man visited our street. He supplied you with a cheque that allowed you to buy stuff. In return you were charged a pretty high rate of interest. Bridget got a Provy Cheque and, on Saturday morning, before the big game, she took me up to Carr's in Easter Road and bought me my first pair of football boots. The match was against St John Vianney's from Gilmerton and I think we had a narrow win. I kept my place and played in the team with Peter until he left for Holy Cross.

St Ninian's had never won anything at football but this was to change in 1955 when we defeated St Bernard's in the final of the EPSSA Cup at Warriston Playing Fields. In the St Bernard's team that day was Davie Whyte who is still a pal and who worked with me forty eight years later when I became manager of Duddingston Golf Club. I am struggling to remember the St Ninian's team but the following definitely played: Dennis Shanley, Stephen Gilhooley, Francis Fallon, James Brannigan, Francis Slater, George McCann, Tom Owens and Willie McLeod. Francis Fallon and Tom Owens have passed away but I still see most of the others now and then. George McCann was a high scoring centre forward and went on to play for Links United and Newtongrange Star. I spent a lot of my early years with George who is the best of company with a razor sharp wit. Just now he is fighting ill health with the determination you would expect. That final is also memorable for me because it was the only time my dad saw me play. He worked away from home much of the time and, when at home, liked to spend his time in his local, "Jock's Lodge". However, that day he made the effort to come and see me play and I could not have been happier.

I had a great disappointment in that I was not selected for the Edinburgh Primary School Team. I got to the final trial at Warriston but played poorly and did not get picked. Wee Joe did not see it that way – he thought it was a "Protestant Plot" to keep me out of the team. Even at twelve I realised that he was wrong; I had not played well enough to be selected.

As well as Wee Joe there were two other teachers who were special to me and who I remember to this day with great fondness. For the last two years at St Ninian's my class teacher was Miss Lamont who looked very old and, until you got to know her, seemed stern. She was unmarried, a proud highlander and a staunch Catholic who had devoted her life to the Virgin Mary. She was "old school" and worked the class hard but underneath she had a soft heart and cared deeply for all her children. I was her "pet" and used to be constantly teased about being the "teacher's pet". I never minded the teasing – I just loved my special status.

The other teacher who lives in my memory is Miss McGuiness. She never taught me but was Peter's teacher. Like Miss Lamont teaching for her was much more than just a job. Once, when Peter was ill, she visited our house to see how he was getting on. Wee Bridget and her became great friends and would occasionally go up town shopping together. Miss McGuiness had complete control of Peter (not easy) and he thought the world of her. What made her exceptional was her passion for music and her determination to make the St Ninian's school choir second to none. As a member of her choir you practised constantly and were driven hard to produce work of the highest quality. Every year we would take part in the competition for schools in the Music Hall in Edinburgh's George Street and every year would win a prize. When our, headteacher, Mr Quigley, died, a requiem mass was held for him in St Ninian's church. At the service the school choir sang the "De Profundis" in Latin. Miss McGuiness was very proud of this. I can hold a tune, but the stars of the choir were Jimmy Casey and George McCann who both had beautiful voices. Many years later, when we were about 35, George arranged for the three of us to visit Miss McGuiness who was now long retired. She made tea for us and we had a great time talking about her choir and its achievements.

In our street, Loganlea Drive, there was little money about. Everybody was poor. If you have never had underpants or sheets on the bed you do not miss them. Take it from me! The main person in the lives of me and all my pals was our mothers. They fussed over us and looked after us; no one more so than my Wee Bridget. The men worked long hours and many of them were like my dad and spent most of their free time in the pub. There was a huge amount of drunkenness that was taken for granted and not frowned upon all that much. The worth of a man was measured by how good a provider he was. Any social events for the children were organised by the mothers. When I was about ten, my mother and her fellow cleaners at the Royal High Primary School took us "doon the water" for the day to Dunoon. We got the train through to Glasgow and then onto the boat. It never stopped raining but I had a great time.

The fact that, when I was a child, the adults I interacted with were mainly women did, I think, influence my attitude to the opposite sex as I grew up. I think women are wonderful; I am happy in their company and I love them. To be fair I am like my dad in that I am more than content to allow my wife to do the housework and feed me and, in case you are wondering, no I do not do my own ironing!

Besides football (and the many street games we played) I had two other main ways of spending my time. In Craigentinny Primary School, at the end of our street, there was a small public library. From a young age I was constantly borrowing books. Biggles, the Hardy Boys, and Enid Blyton were my favourites. My other passion was the cinema. Up the Smoky Brae to Piershill and you were at the Carlton picture house. All of us went there at least once a week. There was always two pictures showing and performances were continuous so that you could stay there as long as you liked. Going in after the start never bothered us and I am still happy to watch films on telly that are half-way through. A crowd of us would go to the Carlton on Saturday afternoons (when the Hibs were away from home) and I can remember Tommy Coyle lining us up in columns of two in 7th Cavalry style to trot down the Smoky Brae and home after watching John Ford's "She Wore a Yellow Ribbon".

In writing about my childhood it is almost impossible to overstate the importance of the Hibernian Football Club to the Christie household. My mother was from a sporting background and used to regale Peter and I with tales of her brother, our Uncle Cornelius (Corny), and the wonderful things he had achieved when playing Gaelic football for County Roscommon. Now that she had made her life in Edinburgh, Hibs, with their Irish background, became her passion; a passion she passed on to her two sons. As a three year old I learned to rhyme off the Hibs team and whenever we had visitors my proud parents would ask me to recite:

Keir

Govan Shaw

Howie Aird Kean

Smith Combe Linwood Turnbull Ormond.

My dad also loved football and, as a young man, went to see the "High Bee's" home and away. It was he who took me to my first Hibs match in 1947 when I was four; we were at home to Queens Park. In goal for Queens that day was 16 year old Ronnie Simpson who later played for Hibs but is best remembered as a 1967 "Lisbon Lion" when he was a member of Jock Stein's great Celtic team who became the first British team to win the European Cup. When he retired from football Ronnie opened a sport's shop in Edinburgh's Rose Street. I used to order the football kit for my schools from him and we became friendly – which for me was a huge thrill. My first match was one of the few times my dad took me to a game because he preferred going with his pals and so it was left to Wee Bridget to take her boys to Easter Road.

At every home game we were in place at the bottom of the slope behind the Leith end goal at least one hour before kick- off. In those days you had to be early because the attendances were massive. The 1950's were great days for Hibs fans who were privileged to watch the "Famous Five": Smith Johnstone Reilly Turnbull Ormond. I grew up thinking that no team could play football like them. Gordon Smith was our hero and we worried about his health and wellbeing as if he was a family member. For me Gordon is the best Scottish player I have seen and I was privileged to train with him and watch him at close quarters when, at the end of his career, he was a member of the 1962 Dundee team that won the league.

Bridget's ambition for me was that I was to be a teacher and she drove me hard. But these were the days before floodlight football and cup replays were on a Wednesday with an afternoon kick-off. She was desperate to see these games but what about her boys' education? Keeping Peter off school was not a problem – he was not going to be a schoolteacher; but having Terence play truant was another thing. Somehow she resolved this dilemma and we never missed a midweek match getting on the special train at Waverley or Haymarket for away games.

The memories of two matches are with me today. 1953 was the year of the Coronation of the Queen and a knock out Coronation Cup was held involving the four best teams in England against the four best in Scotland. The final was at Hampden Park with Hibs playing Celtic and Peter and I were there with Wee Bridget. The "Famous Five" were at their best and ripped Celtic apart for 90 minutes. We lost 2-0 mainly because John Bonnar in the Celtic goal had the best game of his life.

Then there was the heartbreak of 1958 when we were in the Scottish Cup Final against Clyde. Hibs did not have a great team with Eddie Turnbull and Willie Ormond being the only survivors of the "Famous Five" but we did have Joe Baker who was a wonderful centre forward. Again Peter and I were there with Wee Bridget on the terraces of Hampden an hour before kick-off. Early in the match that Clyde villain, Clinton, injured Andy Aitken who played no further part in the game. These were the days before substitutes and we played most of the match with ten men and lost 1-0. The three of us were miserable.

Holy Cross Academy

In 1955 I left my beloved St Ninian's and went to Holy Cross Academy senior secondary school and was there until I left for university in 1961. Writing about my experiences 60 years later is difficult. It was dreadful but it was wonderful; there were cruel teachers but there were kind teachers. It cared only for the brightest pupils and it allowed children to be treated badly.

As a senior secondary school (the equivalent of an English grammar school) it took only pupils who had done well in the qualification exam ("The Qually") that was based on the now largely discredited intelligence tests. The brightest Catholic youngsters from Edinburgh, East Lothian, Midlothian and West Lothian went there and it was an academic hot house.

I almost did not go there. Wee Bridget was determined to do the best for me and she wanted me to sit a test for Edinburgh's prestigious Royal High School that was run by the local authority but was fee paying. The fact that it was not a Catholic school took second place to her desire to do her best for Terence. I did not take the test because the Royal High was a rugby playing school and I wanted to play school's football.

My first day at Holy Cross will always stay with me. Wee Bridget had gone to great lengths to impress on me that it was not going to be like St Ninian's. Peter, who was already there, filled me with terror about how mean the teachers were. He was also determined to lead his wee brother along the right path. With my pals from St Ninian's, Jimmy Casey, Cheswaf Komorovsky and Joe Hegarty I intended to go to school dinners at lunchtime. Peter was having none of that. He marched the four of us to Nairns the baker along at Bonnington Road and showed us how to distract the attention of the woman behind the counter whilst he stole the mince pies.

Because I had done well in the Qually I was placed in the top first year class, 1A, where all our teachers pushed us really hard. It was very competitive which suited me. Every night I had two hours of homework with Wee Bridget supervising me. I studied in my bedroom, which had no heating. Worried about my catching pneumonia she bought me a one bar electric fire. No cost was to be spared in ensuring her boy did well!

Discipline at Holy Cross was harsh – you were belted for any minor infraction. The head of classics was Mr Lappin who was known as "Bunny". For years he abused kids with the approval of the headteacher, Hugh Toner. Bunny kept his leather belt under his academic gown and must have gone home worn out at the end of the day from belting children. You were belted for going up the stairs two at a time; speaking in the playground after you had lined up with your class; touching your cutlery in the dining room before your meal was served and if you were slightly late after lunchtime. Looking back the worse was getting belted if your homework was not up to scratch. Many teachers did this and I recollect being whacked by the head of French, "Froggie", because my ink homework was untidy.

Hugh Toner was in many ways a good man. He wanted his pupils to achieve but the pressure of the job was probably too much for him. Peter was never out of trouble and Mr Toner referred to him as a "gutter snipe" on more than one occasion. Jimmy Casey has been my pal since we met as five year olds at St Ninian's. He is one of nicest people you could meet and was never belted at primary school. He looks back on his days at Holy Cross with horror and remembers being regularly called "gutter snipe" by the headteacher. I used to go to his house in Lochend Gardens to help him with his Latin homework so that Bunny would have no reason to assault him. As I got older I was belted less and it was my impression that decent teachers were under pressure not to appear soft and had to accept the ethos of knocking hell out of the kids.

When I was in sixth year, 18 years old and a part-time professional footballer with Dundee, I was in the sixth year common room at morning interval and was heading a ball against the wall. Not acceptable behaviour, I agree, but then Bunny walked into the room and caught me. He gave me six of the belt, hitting me as hard as he could. I have always regretted holding out my hands and allowing that cruel man to beat me but, in those days, you just did not question people in authority.

However, some of the teachers were terrific. My favourite was Mr Black, the head of English. His sons attended the school and, as well as being an inspiring teacher, he liked children. He had a great sense of humour and somehow he never needed to belt anybody. What a pleasure it was when it was time to go to English. In those days there were no guidance departments in schools and the teachers knew nothing about your background. I remember in my first year when Mr Black told me to stay behind after class and asked me about my parents and what they did. I told him that that my dad was a crane driver and my mother a school cleaner. He asked if Peter was really my brother and I affirmed that he was. After a few minutes he sent me on my way telling me that I was doing well. These words of encouragement meant a great deal to me and when I became a teacher I tried hard to be like Blackie.

The science teachers Mr Holligan, Mr Igoe and Mr Wyatt were in the mould of Mr Black and quickly science became one of my favourite subjects. All the hard work I put in paid dividends and at the end of the first year I was the top pupil in the year and was very proud to receive a prize at the annual prize giving in the Usher Hall.

One of the pupils in my class was a friendly and full of fun boy called Patrick Wheatley who invited some of his classmates, including me, to his birthday party at his home. Nothing very special about that, but Patrick's dad was Lord Wheatley who, at the time, was Scotland's

Lord Advocate and who later went on to become Baron Wheatley. Before becoming a judge Lord Wheatley was a MP and represented Edinburgh East where we lived. He was a member of the Labour party and a hero to my mum and dad. It was with great trepidation that I got off the number five tram outside their posh house in the Grange close to Morningside. My worries were groundless as we had a great time playing lots of games all organised by Lord Wheatley. After first year, Patrick left Holy Cross to go to boarding school and when he left school became a lawyer, like his dad, as did his older brother John who sits on the bench as Lord Wheatley.

In second year my foot came slightly off the accelerator and I was runner up to a girl called Ann Gavin. After that I went into reverse for a couple of years and was a spectator when it came to receiving prizes at the Usher Hall.
At the end of fourth year, after the prize giving, Mr Igoe took me aside and gave me a bit of a dressing down and told me that, if I got back to working hard, I would be dux of the school at the end of fifth year, I took his advice to heart and once again the one bar electric fire in my bedroom was working overtime. Towards the end of the school year Mr Toner came into my classroom and asked to speak to me out in the corridor. He told me that I was dux of the school and I could not wait to get home and tell Wee Bridget. It was a great thrill to receive my dux medal from Archbishop Grey at the prize giving in the Usher Hall watched by my mum, dad and Peter who were dressed in their Sunday best. It

would have been nice to have a picture of that happy occasion but we could not afford a camera.

In spite of the cruelty of a minority of the teachers I did love the six years I spent at Holy Cross. What I loved best was the school football! The football teacher was John Coleman who was head of art and wore a beret. Every day after school, legend had it that he headed for the Abbotsford pub in Rose Street and stayed there until closing. Helping him with the football were science teachers Willie Wyatt and Luke Igoe. Mind you at one point it looked like I was not going in the team. The trials for the first year team were held one Saturday morning at Arboretum Playing Fields with Willie Wyatt and Luke Igoe in charge. There were about 40 of us desperate to catch the eye and become members of the top team, which was called the "B's". I had been captain of my primary school team and thought I was a "shoo in" to get selected. The teachers picked two teams and threw a ball to those not chosen and told them to have a kick about on the neighbouring pitch. My name had not been called out and for the next half hour I aimlessly kicked a ball about with the other rejects. I was livid! I got on at half-time and showed these teachers just how wrong they had been to leave me out! As a teenager I played in Edinburgh juvenile football against the likes of Rangers legends John Greig and Willie Henderson and, as a 17 year old, trained at Dundee with Alan Gilzean and Gordon Smith. Playing with such great players gave me an appreciation of my position in the pecking order and it did not take long for me to realise that my best route to making something of myself was the academic one and not that of a professional footballer. However, as a twelve year old I thought I was something special and was not keen to forgive Messrs Wyatt and Igoe for ignoring me. I did get selected for the "B's" and had three happy, happy years playing for my school.

At that time at Holy Cross there were a number of boys who went on to become professional footballers. Chief amongst them was Pat Stanton, the captain of Eddie Turnbull's 1972 League Cup winning Hibs team. That day Hibs beat Celtic 2-1 at Hampden with Pat and Jimmy O'Rourke getting the goals. I could not be at the game because I was playing for Stirling Albion. The following Saturday (my 29th birthday) our match was postponed and, with my great friend and mentor, fellow Hibs fanatic, Tam Mclaren, I was on the Easter Road terraces to see Hibs annihilate Ayr United 8-1 and give the best performance I have ever seen from a Hibs team.

Pat was the year below me at Holy Cross but we first met some years before when, for a short time, he and I were in the Cubs together at St Ninian's. Pat attended St Francis primary school in Craigmillar and was encouraged to join St Ninian's Cubs by his teacher, Joe Dykes who was the cubmaster. In my opinion Pat is second only to my hero, Gordon Smith, in the list of greatest ever Hibs players. The triangle down the right side of John Brownlie, Alex Edwards and Pat Stanton produced some of the finest football I have ever seen played by Hibs. One goal Pat scored sticks in my mind.

He was basically an old fashioned wing half but he could get forward to great effect. For this goal he played the ball to Alex Edwards on the right wing and ran past him; Alex could place the ball on a sixpence and on this occasion he did just that. It dropped over Pat's right shoulder and he volleyed it into net as if it was routine. It pleased me greatly that, when he left Hibs, Pat signed for Celtic and won a league champions medal with them playing at centre back.

At lunchtime we would bolt down our school dinner and run to the adjoining Victoria Park for a game of football. Often we would arrive back at school slightly late and, of course, get belted. As well as Pat Stanton I remember playing football in the park with the following: George Brough (Hibs); Tony McGlynn (Hibs); Jimmy O'Rourke (Hibs legend!); Davie Hogg (Hibs and Dundee United); Jimmy McManus (Dundee United); and Denis Devlin who played in goal for Falkirk. One of the best players at the school was my great pal, Andy Johnstone, who would have become a professional player if he had not decided to pursue a career as a navigator with the Royal Air Force.

When I was in third year, aged 14, I was picked to play at Tynecastle in the final trial for the Edinburgh Secondary Schools team. Also playing that day were John Greig and Roy Barry who went on to play for Hearts, Coventry and Dunfermline. I was selected for the squad, which was a great thrill after not making the Edinburgh Primary School team. It would be stretching the truth if I were to pretend that I was a first pick for the side; that was not the case, as the teachers in charge often preferred bigger and stronger lads.

One game does stick in my mind. Every year Edinburgh played Sheffield. In 1957 it was our turn to travel and we played at Sheffield Wednesday's ground, Hillsborough, under floodlights, which were just starting to be introduced. I remember the match for other than football reasons. At the hotel in which we were staying the lift was operated by a buxom girl who was more than willing when it came to sticking the lips on the faces of the eager schoolboys from "Auld Reekie". No journey in a lift has ever been quite the same!

As a 15 year old I learned a lesson about being on time. At the end of every season there was a six-a-side competition at Meggetland in the Craiglockhart part of the city – a good distance from our school on Ferry Road. Our team was allowed away early from school so that we would arrive in good time for the early afternoon start of the tournament. Four of us decided that, since time was plentiful, we should stop for a quick game of snooker in Leith Street. We spent an eternity trying to pot the black and when we got off the tram at Meggetland the tournament was already underway. We were too late to take part. Our teacher Mr Coleman was seething with anger and the situation was not helped by our makeshift team being narrowly defeated in the final. In the 43 years I was involved in professional football as a player and manager I was never again late for a match. A lesson had been learned the hard way.

Ten years later in 1968, having been teaching for two years, I refereed the final of that tournament. I remember not refereeing the match particularly well because I was distracted by the outstanding level of skill being shown by a boy who was playing for Carrickvale School. He questioned every decision I made and seemed more of a man than a young boy. This was the one and only time I shared a pitch with Graeme Souness and it is memory I treasure.

I left Holy Cross in 1961 to study Chemistry at Edinburgh University, and was determined to be a teacher but also keen to pursue a career as a part-time footballer – I had signed for Dundee in October 1960 aged 17.

Before finishing this chapter there are two things I should mention. First is my role as a model in the art department, which I fulfilled for most of my six years at school. I would be taken out of class by Mr Coleman, stripped to the waist with my PE kit on, and sit for hours whilst the pupils doing Higher Art drew me. I used to thing I had been selected because of my regular features and manly little body until one day Mr Coleman announced to the class: "If you can draw Christie's head, you can draw anything." As you know I am deformed.

No account of my time at Holy Cross would be complete without telling you about Mary Boyle. In our sixth year Mary and I became very friendly and I walked her home from the Christmas dance. She lived nearby in Ferry

Road. Mary was smart, beautiful and a truly special girl. I thought the world of her. Nothing came of our budding romance but whenever I think of my days at Holy Cross I always think of the part Mary Boyle played in my life.

Dundee FC

It was toward the end of my third year at Holy Cross when an older pupil, Victor Rickis, asked me if I wanted to train with the juvenile team Edinburgh Norton who were Scottish champions just having won the Lord Weir Cup. Victor was a member of that cup winning team and he left Edinburgh Norton to play for Millwall. I could not have been more pleased at getting the chance to join such an illustrious team. They were based beside me in the Abbeyhill district of Edinburgh and had good men running them.

Just before I joined them two Abbeyhill legends had played for Norton – Willie Hunter and Bobby Roberts; and I became great friends with both of them. Willie was the quintessential Scottish footballer – small, fast and tricky; he glided over the ground. Willie left Norton when he was seventeen to join Motherwell and played on the right wing for the best team in the history of that club. They had a wonderful front five: Hunter, Reid, St John, Quinn, and Weir. The manager of Motherwell at the time was Bobby Ancell and his team was known as the "Ancell Babes". As well as their attackers they also had two outstanding wing halves - Bert McCann and Charlie Aitken. Although he was playing in one of Scotland's most successful clubs Willie for several years was a part-time player working in an Edinburgh stockbroker office. He often trained with the Norton and in some ways took me under his wing. I remember when he told me that I had to do something about my hair, which, at the time, was a tangled mess. He suggested that I visit Charlie Miller who had a barber's shop in Prestonfield. I did as instructed and left the shop with a fashionable "Perry Como". Willie played for Hibs and later managed Queen of the South and Inverness Caley. It pleased me greatly that he regularly brought his dad to see Meadowbank Thistle when I was the manager. He is an original thinker about football and I learned much from him.

Bobby Roberts and Willie were brought up together. Willie was reared in Beggs Buildings and Bobby in the close-by Milton Street. Although they were best pals they were very different characters. Willie was cerebral whilst Bobby operated more on instinct. Willie 'glided over the ground' whilst Bobby did not "glide" but was ultra competitive and a born winner. He was a midfielder who scored goals. Like Willie he left Norton for Motherwell. Bobby felt he had to look after me. I had just joined Dundee and was playing against a Motherwell reserve team and I noticed, as the game progressed, that none of the opposition were tackling me. Bobby was playing for Motherwell that day and it dawned on me that his teammates were following his instructions to go easy on me. He left Motherwell to join Leicester City for whom he played 230 games and for whom he is something of a legend. After playing he managed Colchester, Wrexham and Grimsby and then became a football scout and, as you read this, is probably at a match seeking out tomorrow's star. I have not seen Bobby for many years but his commitment to doing your best and winning greatly influenced me. He was warm, he was interested in you and he became a role model for me.

Back to 1958 and making sure I became a regular in the Edinburgh Norton team. Prior to joining Norton I had always played in midfield. It was a position that allowed me to play to my strengths: I had a high work rate, seldom gave the ball away and I was competitive. On the down side I had a nervous breakdown when given the chance to score and could be overpowered by bigger boys. The obvious solution was to play me as a winger; the problem for me was that I had above average pace but not enough to be a success as a winger – unless the fullback was hopeless. In defence of myself I should say that I was a very good crosser of the ball and had spent endless hours as a kid improving my left foot. If the left back shut me down I could pull the ball back to my left foot and put the ball into the "danger area". It drives me crazy nowadays when multi-millionaires are unable to deliver the ball into the penalty box; hitting the first defender with the ball has become the norm!

Yes you are right; the men who ran Edinburgh Norton decided to play me as a right or left-winger. But then I was dropped from the team! I was distraught and ran home – the match was at Holyrood Park, not too distant from where I lived. On seeing me in tears my dad decided to take positive action! Against my will we went back to the scene of my humiliation. Bobby Lancaster was the manager of the team and although it is totally irrelevant I have to tell you that, like me, he was vertically challenged. My powerfully built dad had a few direct words with wee Bobby and never again was I left out of the Norton team. As a left wing liberal even today I struggle to come to terms with my dad's methods – but I loved the outcome.

Norton were a good side but not the best team in Edinburgh; that title belonged to Edinburgh Athletic who, under the management of Syd Brydon, had put together a team of the best young players in Scotland. Willie Henderson was the star in a team that included Alex Willoughby (Rangers); Alan Gordon (Hearts, Hibs Dundee United , Dundee and one of my favourite all time players); and Tommy Murray who was a wee star for Hearts and Airdrie. In my second season with Norton I played against John Greig and Eric Stevenson. When we played together with Edinburgh schools John had been a wee guy – like me. He was now a giant and playing at a level away above anything I could match. Eric (Hibs' legend) had more control of the football than anybody I had ever seen. I remember a cup final when he had the ball at the corner flag and I was in close proximity. It was impossible for him to get past me with the ball - he did – and that explains why he is in the Hibs' "Hall of Fame".

In my second season with Norton I had a trial with Falkirk but nothing came of it. I went on to play for the Norton under -21 team although I was still just 17. I was still a winger, which I hated, but fortunately there were few good fullbacks in Edinburgh juvenile football in 1960. I played outside left or outside right. I preferred outside left, not only because, being right footed, I found it easier to beat an opponent who would allow me to come inside, but because our left back tackled like a demon and was happy to give the ball to me. That man was Lawrie Glasson. All of you reading this have good friends; but none of you have a better friend than Lawrie. He would do anything for me. In our 55 year old relationship I have been the taker and writing this gives me the chance to say how much I love and appreciate him.

At the start of the 1960 season Norton were in great form. Our centre forward, Stan Vincent, who went on to play for Hibs, was a goal machine and we were regularly thumping every team we played. I was playing on the wing and revelling in the lack of pace of opposition full-backs. At a Saturday game at Woods Park in Portobello I noticed that Dundee coach, Sammy Kean (ex Hibee) was on the touchline. I became nervous and allowed the first pass to me to roll under my foot. After that I was a man possessed and played the best game of my life.

On Sunday, I was contacted by one of the men who ran Norton to tell me that I was to meet the Dundee Manager, Bob Shankly, on Monday at Binns' corner in Princes Street. At the meeting Bob Shankly was accompanied by Sammy Kean and Dundee's Edinburgh scout, Davie Dalziel who had the doubtful distinction of spotting me. The meeting went well and I agreed to sign on a part-time basis; I was still determined to go to university and become a teacher. I did not put pen to paper there and then because I felt that, for such a big step, I needed my dad's approval and he was working in Arbroath building a school. It was agreed that I would meet Bob Shankly in Dundee in two days time and that he would drive me to Arbroath to meet my dad. Everything worked out fine and in October 1960, a couple of months away from my 18th birthday, I became a professional footballer.

Back then it was not that common for a 17 year old to sign for a top club (as Dundee were in 1960) and my photograph was in several newspapers with the result that I became a little bit full of myself with the metaphorical dimensions of my head just about matching its actual size.

My signing for Dundee resulted in a significant change in my life at school. Although I was strong in science and maths, I was the top pupil in the school at History and the Principal Teacher of History, Jimmy Dolan, had persuaded me to take the entrance exam for Oxford University to study History and follow in the footsteps of Norah Carlin who had been the dux of the school the year before me. Norah had a successful career in the History Department of Middlesex University and has written a history of Holy Cross Academy. Playing for Dundee whilst a student at Oxford was not practical and so that was the end of me as an historian although I have retained a lifelong interest in the subject. I have to admit to a certain relief at abandoning the study of feudal life in medieval England.

My first game for Dundee was for the reserves in Glasgow against Third Lanark. I was instructed to be at the Ivanhoe Hotel for lunch and I made sure that I got an early train from the Waverley Station and arrived in good time. When I walked into the hotel I met a young fresh face lad a couple of years older than me, supporting a crew cut, who introduced himself as Craig Brown. He was on loan to Dundee from Rangers and like me was punctual and part-time; he was studying to be a Physical Education teacher at Glasgow's Jordanhill College where his dad, "Bomber Brown" was the principal. A lifelong friendship had started.

The game itself was uneventful but I remember being shown by Albert Henderson, prior to the match, how to properly wear shin pads; Albert was nearing the end of his playing career and in 1962 he became manager of Arbroath for the next 17 years. He was a tough old pro who went out of his way to be kind and helpful to me.

A couple of weeks after signing Bob Shankly asked me if I could take a couple of days of school and stay overnight and train with the full-time players. Hugh Toner, my headteacher, gave permission and early one Tuesday morning, suitcase in hand, I boarded the train for Dundee. All the players were very friendly and welcoming but later in the shower I overheard two of them talking about me. "What do you think of wee Christie?" "Aye, no a bad wee player, but his mother must be missing him from the mantelpiece."

My digs at were at Barnes Avenue with Mrs Garvie with whom several of the young players lived. Billy MacMillan, who lodged there, was given the job of taking me into the city centre for a pair of new boots. A buxom girl was serving us and to my amazement Billy grabbed my head and starting rubbing my face into her ample breasts. I was mortified but the young lady was in no way put out saying to Billy "Behave yourself you are embarrassing the wee lad". I was happy to get out of the shop but thoroughly enjoyed the experience.

I had to share a bed with Billy and was a wee bit nervous about this even though it was obvious that he was a rampant heterosexual. I found getting to sleep difficult but Billy had no such problem. He was tossing and turning and I said goodbye to any chance of sleep when he turned over and started to cuddle into me. It was a long night!

Over the next five years I spent a lot of time in Dundee training with the full-timers during the long holidays from university. I loved rubbing shoulders with so many great players and it is a joy to look back on those very happy days.

The following team won the league in 1962:

Liney

Hamilton Cox

Seith Ure Wishart

Smith Penman Cousin Gilzean Robertson.

The only others to play in the first team that season were Alex Stuart, Bobby Waddell, George McGeachie and Craig Brown.

Here are some personal memories of these Dundee greats:

Pat Liney was not tall for a keeper but had a safe pair of hands and was the friendliest guy you could meet.

Alex Hamilton was a wonderful right back. He was exceptionally quick and a great passer of the ball. He was always up for a laugh and I remember him giving me a hard time one morning at training after I had not starred in a reserve game the previous night. At a football club you have to be able to stand up for yourself and I pointed out to him that I was going to be a scientist and would have the letters BSc after my name. He went quiet for a little while and then came back with "I've got letters after my name". Taking the bait I said, "What letters do you have after your name?" "WCF" he replied. "What does WCF stand for?" I asked. "World Class Full-back" was the reply. Game, set and match to Hammy.

Bobby Cox was the captain of the team and led by example. He was a street fighter who had got where he was by hard work and application and by God he was not going to give it up easily. Like Hamilton he was small and quick and, although not as good on the ball as Hammy, he was a better tackler and few wingers got the better of him. I used to play directly against him in training matches and was frankly intimidated by him. I dribbled past him once and a few quiet words from him convinced me that a repetition was not a good idea. It is fitting that one of the stands at Dens Park is named after him.

Bobby Seith anchored the midfield and he was exceptionally strong, secure in possession and a great passer of the ball. He seldom got ahead of the ball but was adept at breaking up attacks and using the ball to advantage. He was a keen thinker on football and in my later time at Dundee I thoroughly enjoyed the coaching he did with the reserve team.

Ian Ure was a star; although only two years older than me he was already established in the first team when I joined the club. He was quite a sight with his mop of blonde hair and was exceptionally fast for such a tall lad. Ian had a great work ethic and often stayed behind to practise on his own. I followed his career with great interest when he left Dundee and joined Arsenal and later Manchester United.

Bobby Wishart was one of manager Bob Shankly's best signings. He had been a successful player with Aberdeen who made a mistake in transferring him to Dundee in January 1961. He was a talented player who could dribble and shoot with a left foot that did his bidding - he was a regular scorer. Like me he lived in

Edinburgh and was part-time and I frequently travelled with him on the train from Edinburgh. Bobby was friendly and willing to help young players. I valued his advice and he was very much a mentor to me. Towards the end of his time with Dundee he played in the reserves and was greatly encouraging and had the knack of telling you where you were going wrong in a manner that did not knock the feet from you – a difficult thing to do. During the close season I golfed with him at Baberton Golf Club where he is still a member. Bobby was an astute man and I was not the only player who sought his advice. When Alan Gilzean was being transferred to Tottenham Hotspur his advisor was Bobby who had a financial background and was wise in money matters. A parable of Bobby's always stuck with me; it was about the husband who takes his wife out for lunch every Sunday and then one Sunday asks if he can go golfing. The wife was not best pleased! He compared that situation to the husband who golfs every Sunday and then one week announces that he is not golfing but is taking his spouse out for lunch. That man is a hero!

Gordon Smith was my hero as a child and remained my hero when I became an adult. He was the star of the Hibs' "Famous Five": Smith Johnstone Reilly Turnbull and Ormond and won league championship medals with Hibs, Hearts and Dundee. He was tall, handsome, fast, skilled and had an elegance about everything he did. He joined Dundee a few months after me and I was thrilled that I was to be a teammate of the "Gay Gordon" even though his signing further lengthened the odds of my getting a game in the first team; by the time he signed I was the regular outside right in the reserve team – Gordon was also an outside right but just a wee bit more talented than me! He lived in North Berwick and occasionally I would travel on the train with him to Dundee. Gordon was shy and reserved but always polite and kind. He was extremely careful about what he ate and the only time I saw him get a little techy was when he was having a discussion with George McGeachie about the merits of unrefined sugar as compared to refined sugar. George was a part-time player, had a degree in chemistry and worked as a chemist in the refinery at Grangemouth. He therefore new a little about the chemistry of sugars and he was definite in his view that any difference was purely superficial. Gordon was having none of that and became quite animated in putting forward the case for unrefined sugar. The first team players told the story of when they were playing Sporting Lisbon in Portugal in the European Cup. The quiet Gordon surprised everybody at half-time by suggesting that Andy Penman could exploit the space behind their left back who was man marking Gordon. Bob Shankly, the manager, liked to "keep things simple" and his reaction to Gordon's suggestion was, "For fuck's sake Gordon didnae get complicated".

Many years after my time at Dundee I took my Meadowbank Thistle team to Dens Park. We won the match 1-0 thanks to an Ian Little goal. In the board room after the game I was delighted to meet Bobby Wishart and Gordon who were present as guests of their old club. I chatted with them recalling old days when they were asked to go to one of the lounges to meet some fans. I said my farewells to them but Gordon was having none of it. " Terry, you were part of things back then and so are coming with us". I was embarrassed and tried to get out of it but he insisted and I accompanied them. The consideration shown to me by Gordon was a measure of the man and confirmed him as a hero in my eyes.

Andy Penman satisfied both of the criteria to merit the description "a dour Fifer"; he was from Fife and he was most definitely dour. But he also was a great footballer. He had a wonderful right foot and was a regular scoring in the championship winning Dundee team. Andy was younger than me and I was in awe of him. When I watched him train and play it was obvious to me that he was at a level I could never reach. In their right channel Dundee had three exceptional players – Alex Hamilton, Gordon Smith and Andy Penman.

Alan Cousin signed as a 17 year old for Dundee in 1955 and was a part-timer for the 10 years he was at the club. After studying Latin and Greek at St Andrews University he went on to teach classics in his native Clackmannanshire. His striking partnership with Alan Gilzean was hugely successful and he scored lots of goals but not as many as the prolific "Gilly". When Alan left Dundee he played for Hibs and then Falkirk and he and I were opponents when Falkirk played Stirling Albion around 1970. Stirling won that day and that's maybe why I remember the game.

Alan Gilzean was the star of that best ever Dundee team. Not only was he a great goal scorer he was also a terrific all round player with skills that were well embedded. He was a powerful rather than speedy runner but he could score with either foot and was unbeatable in the air. Gilly was five or so years older than me but he was friendly and interested in the younger players and I both admired and liked him. In November 1962 he scored seven goals in a 10-2 victory over Queen of the South. I was sitting at the lunch table a few days later when he asked me if I wanted to go back to Dens Park for some additional practice. I readily agreed and that afternoon the two of us were out on the pitch ourselves with numerous footballs when he said to me, "You know Terry it's no that difficult knocking it into the top corner from outside the box". Well, for me it was more than difficult but not for Gilly who, from 25 yards or so, proceeded to clip ball after ball into the postage stamp corner of the goal.

At the end of the 1963/64 season he was out of contract and refused to resign for Dundee who were understandably reluctant to see him leave – in those "pre Bosman" days players who were out of contact could be "retained" by the club. A new season started and he was training but was not eligible to play in competitive matches. Eventually manager, Bob Shankly, admitted defeat and Gilly resigned on the understanding that he would be transferred. His first game back was in the reserves at Kilmarnock with representatives of most of England's top clubs in attendance. A feature of Dundee's success was Gilly's partnership with Gordon Smith who was one of the finest crossers of the ball I have ever seen – on a par with David Beckham but Gordon was fast and could also dribble unlike the tattooed idol. Back to Rugby Park in November 1964; Gilly's future depended on how well he did that day and cast in the Gordon Smith roll was Edinburgh University student, Terry Christie.

The ball came to me on the wing and Gilly made his way to the back post. Get it to him and it was a goal! Unfortunately I miscued and the ball went behind the goal for a goal kick. Minutes later I was given another chance to set him up but this time I stubbed my foot in the ground and the ball ran only a few yards. The pressure was getting to Gilly so much so that he shouted over to me, "For fuck's sake Terry, you'll have me in the fucking Highland League." Fortunately things brightened up; he scored three goals and within a few day signed for Tottenham Hotspur and became one of that famous club's legends.

Hugh Robertson was a native of Ayrshire and was outgoing and hugely likeable. He was also a wee bit of a rogue. At the start of a new season I was due a new pair of boots when Hugh persuaded me that I should wear his fairly old boots so as to allow him to get another brand new pair. I agreed and spent some time playing in boots that were a poor fit and probably played a part in my demise. Sucker! Religion and the Protestant/Catholic divide were a constant source of ribbing at the club. Once when Hugh was getting on to me for being a "wee Pape" I explained to him that we had much in common, since we were both Christians. His retort was, " I'm no a fuckin Christian, I'm a Proddy". Hugh was a terrific left winger who had great control of the ball and linked well particularly with Gilzean.

The above eleven were Dundee's regular team and only four other players played in the league winning side: George McGeachie, Alex Stuart, Bobby Waddell and Craig Brown.

Like me George McGeachie was part-time working (as I have mentioned) as a chemist at Grangemouth. He was a tricky winger and it was only the arrival of Gordon Smith that saw him demoted from the first team.

I spent quite a bit of time in digs with Alex Stuart and he helped me greatly by being kind and encouraging. He was a strong powerful player and would have played in most first teams at the time. When he finished playing he went on to manage St Johnstone and Ayr United.

Like Alex, Bobby Waddell was another older player who looked after me. We were friends and I greatly admired his openness and honesty but he was also warm and good company. Bobby was a prolific scorer in the reserves but never managed to repeat his scoring form in the first team. I loved playing with him – as a winger you just needed get the ball in the box and there was a good chance the Bobby would put it in the net. He later played for East Fife and I remember playing against him for Stirling Albion and Bobby being amazed that I was captain of the Stirling team; "You're no the Captain!". (One of the few occasions that I captained any team.)

Craig Brown was probably the Dundee player that had most influence on me. In my five years there we became great friends and remain so. Craig had been brought up in a "bought hoose" in Hamilton and, although he would hate me saying this, he was close to being middle class. His dad, Bomber Brown, was an educated man and he made sure that his three sons were also well educated. One of the huge differences between Craig and I at the time was that he spoke grammatically and was always correcting me because I found it difficult to put together two grammatically correct words. He was great fun but was also wise beyond his years and I tried to follow his example of behaving well and doing the right thing. He had a huge love of football and, given his passion for the game and his intelligence and strength of character, it was no surprise to me that he was a very successful manager of our national team.

As well as the above league winners there were other players who were good friends of mine and I remember them with great affection: Tommy Mackle; Doug Houston; Jim Duthie; Norman Beattie; Hugh Reid; George Ryden; Ally Donaldson and Kenny Cameron who scored a great goal in the 1964 Scottish cup final against Rangers. In my latter years three younger players, who went on to have great careers, became teammates: George Stewart, Steve Murray and Jocky Scott.

Dundee's success was mainly because of their talented players but in Bob Shankly they also had a good manager. Bob was the older brother of Liverpool's Bill Shankly but did not have any of his sibling's ready humour and quick wit. But he was a hard task master and made sure that his players gave of their best. He demanded high standards and at half-time was not shy in naming those who needed to improve. Nobody messed with him but he was fair, straightforward and had the respect of all the players. He had a strong belief that football was about skill and encouraged his team to play a passing game. At training he was always emphasising "pass and move" and this showed in the way his team performed. He was not one for always making with the jokes but after a good away win he would quote a legendary Scottish manager Willie McCartney: "As Willie McCartney would say let's get the fuck oot it here" and then almost laugh.

In my time at Dundee I had two injuries that stayed with me all my life. After a few months of signing, my right shoulder dislocated and continued to dislocate with great regularly. When I was 20 I had a bone graft operation to fix it. Although much improved, it dislocated a couple of times after the operation and, although I continued to play for many years, I tended to make sure that I never did anything overhand with my right arm including taking a throw-in. My second serious injury occurred in my last game for Dundee - the reserve cup final against Rangers. Before the match one of the Rangers' defenders, Roger Hynd, who was massive, asked me to pick my seat in the stand. He was joking, but after about 20 minutes a tackle from him resulted in my tearing the ligaments in my knee, which is now badly arthritic.

In 1965 Bob Shankly left for Hibernian and Bobby Ancell became manager and let me go. It was a great disappointment but I knew in my heart of hearts that I was not good enough.

University. Love and Marriage

In 1960, towards the end of my fifth year at Holy Cross, I met Margaret Ferguson; she was 14 and I was 17. I was immediately smitten and for the next five years she was my girlfriend until we married in 1965. Like all romances everything was not plane sailing and over our five year courtship there were short periods when we decided to have a break from each other. Margaret's background was quite different from mine in that her parents, Molly and Jock, had a fairly large house in nearby Portobello and occasionally took in lodgers; Molly looked after the house and Jock was a driving instructor. Molly had been brought up on a farm near Carlisle and Jock was originally a Dundonian. They were good people and I got on great with both of them.

Margaret was beautiful and I was very taken with her. She left Portobello High School at 15 and went to work in Jenners in Princes Street as a trainee beautician. She was a born saleswoman and was in retail all her working life. Throughout our courtship we saw each other a couple of times a week at most because I was busy training and studying.

In 1961 I started my chemistry course at Edinburgh University. I had made up my mind that I wanted to be a teacher and university and chemistry were the means to this end. I pondered long before deciding to do chemistry rather than mathematics but finally plumbed for chemistry because I thought it might be less demanding and allow me more time for football. I maybe got that wrong!

Many talk about university as a live changing experience but that was not the case with me. Balancing professional football and studying meant that I had four years of hard graft. I made it harder for myself because I rewrote every lecture. My writing is big and loopy and my lecture notes were a mess and so at home I would rewrite the notes adding relevant points from textbooks – no computers back then. When you study a science you spend a lot of time doing experiments in a laboratory – for me this was a problem. I am completely handless and none of my experiments worked. The afternoons I spent in a chemistry lab were the most miserable of my life. How did I get through? Well, I cannot reveal that but a great deal of cunning and deviousness were involved.

My ambition was that one-day I might become the head of a chemistry department in a school, like Mr Holligan, the principal teacher of chemistry at Holy Cross, whom I greatly admired. In order to get to those lofty heights you had to have an honours degree and, in order to get into final honours year, the fourth year, you had to do well in third year. Football was put on the back burner and I swatted like never before, so much so that I finished third in a year containing over a hundred students. Very proud! However in my final year the work rate reduced drastically and I graduated in 1965 with a second-class honours degree and have regretted all my life that I did not put in the effort to get a first.

On 25 June 1965 Margaret and I were married in St Ninian's church with nuptial mass. I was a fairly devout Catholic and I was delighted when Margaret decided to convert to Catholicism. Looking back, I suppose I did put a bit pressure on her but I think it is a decision that she has never regretted. We bought a little flat in Waverly Park using money I had saved from my earnings at Dundee. For my last three years there I was paid £14.00 per week, which was more than my dad was earning. Because I was working I did not receive a grant when I was at university but compared to my fellow students I was well off and Wee Bridget made sure that I saved every penny. The flat was just over £1,400 and I was able to pay for most of it from the money I had put away. Waverley Park was the perfect location – it overlooked Holyrood Palace and, more important for me, several football pitches on which I spent a great deal of time in the early years of married life. In my defence I have to point out that I was only 22 when I got married (Margaret was just 19) and there was still a lot of the "wee laddie" in me. The youngsters who lived in our street were regularly ringing our doorbell to see if I was "coming oot for a game" - usually I was. My own children often ask me why Margaret and I married so young. In 1965 the "swinging sixties" had most definitely not reached my part of Edinburgh and the "pill" was not yet in widespread use. Sex before marriage was not something good girls indulged in with the result that most of us back then got married very young.

In the first year of married life Margaret was working full-time in Jenners in Princes Street and I was doing a post-graduate teaching course at Edinburgh's Moray House. Because of the post-war boom in births there was a shortage of teachers and Moray House was bursting at the seams. The place was a shambles; I worked a nine-hour week and was one of the more conscientious students. I recollect a tutor observing me on teaching practice and advising me that, "You will never get away with being so friendly to the pupils". Advice I chose to ignore. The best thing that happened to me at Moray House was meeting a fellow student, Joe McDermott. He was from Wishaw and was full of fun and good nature. We became firm friends and remain so.

The start of the 1965-66 football season loomed and I was without a club having been released by Dundee. I had spent the summer recovering from the Roger Hynd tackle and working in Hendry's lemonade factory in Lower London Road. I was invited by George Farm, manager of Raith Rovers, to play in a trial match at Stark's Park and did well enough to be offered a part-time contract. Rovers were a top Second Division team at the time and had some really good players. Celtic legend Bobby Evans was centre half and in midfield they had Ian Porterfield who scored for Sunderland when they defeated Leeds United in the 1973 cup-final at Wembley. He was a terrific player as were Pat Gardner and Willie McLean, brother of Dundee United's great manager, Jim.

I played poorly for Raith and was more out of the team than in it. To play well you have to feel part of things and I never settled at Raith Rovers. I was the only player from Edinburgh and took the train to Kirkcaldy for training two nights a week. The manager was George Farm who had played in goal for Blackpool in the 1953 "Matthews Final" at Wembley. I thought him a bully and never warmed to him; as a coach he was of the "could nae teach dogs to bark" variety. My first training session at Stark's Park set off alarm bells. I was instructed to cross balls from the wing into the goal area with no goalkeeper in place. Instead two full-backs were standing on the goal-line and their job was to meet the cross and kick the ball, as far as they could, down the park to nobody; we did this for 30 minutes by which time the manager seemed satisfied that the full-backs had mastered that difficult skill. I do remember playing against Celtic at Parkhead and being mightily impressed by a team that a couple of years later was to go down in football history as the "Lisbon Lions".

As the 1965-66 season drew to a close I was thoroughly miserable at Raith Rovers and was approached by Willie MacFarlane to play for Hawick Royal Albert in the East of Scotland League. George Farm agreed to release me although I had to fight hard for the money I was due. I signed for Hawick for a small wage and for the next 15 years Willie MacFarlane was a close friend until I ended the friendship with an act of treachery.

Willie was 13 years older than me but the age difference did not prevent us becoming good friends. He had played full-back for Hibs in the mid-fifties when the "Famous Five" were at their peak and I was a ready listener to his tales of what it was like to play alongside my boyhood heroes. Back in those days most full-backs were of the hard-tackling variety and Willie was proud to be in that category. He used to describe with relish how everything seemed to slow down just as he was about to crunch the winger and boasted how three opponents had ended up in hospital on three successive Saturdays. But he had a great sense of humour and it was fun to be around him and I just loved his company.

Professional football was not proceeding as I had hoped but I was looking forward to the start of my teaching career. I graduated from Moray House in the summer of 1966 and set about trying to find a full-time job as a chemistry teacher. During the summer I took a temporary job with Leith Provident Co-op driving one of their bread-vans around Edinburgh's Clermiston housing scheme. Because I was working I could not get near a television to see England defeat Germany in the World Cup final.

One Sunday morning I was coming out of mass at St Ninian's when I was approached by Tom O'Malley who had been several years ahead of me at Holy Cross. Tom was now working as a chemistry teacher at Holy Cross and had been asked to let me know that there was a vacancy for a chemistry teacher at St. David's High School in Dalkeith. The good old "Catholic Mafia" was alive and well! I applied for the post, was successful (surprise) and in August 1966, aged 23, I started my career as a teacher.

St David's took all the Catholic kids from Midlothian and the school had just moved into a brand new building (now demolished.) To my great pleasure my pal from Moray House, Joe McDermott, had got a job there teaching English.

I went into teaching with a clear idea of what kind of teacher I would be. One of my friends at university was Kenny McLeod from Broxburn in West Lothian. Like me, Kenny had his mind made up to be a chemistry teacher and he and I agreed that we were going to be different from the teachers who had taught us. The main thing was that we were not going to be "posh" like nearly all our teachers were but were going to be much more "normal" in the way we related to our pupils who would be in no doubt that we inhabited the same world as them. We would always be "in charge" but in much the same way as our parents had been in charge of us.

From the start I loved being a teacher. If you are extrovert closing the door of your classroom and having twenty impressionable youngsters forced to listen to you is heaven! My reputation in the school was enhanced when in one of my early lessons there was an explosion when my idea of placing a large piece of potassium in a trough of water went badly wrong. Fortunately, no one was injured but for months my pupils would implore, "Sir, go and dae that one with the potassium again".

Because I had a degree in chemistry I was entitled to call myself a "scientist" but I was incapable of doing anything practical. A few weeks into my career I was required to show my class how to use the new fangled electric balance that the chemistry department had just purchased. I went cold all over when my principal teacher told me, "All you have to do is put a plug on it." I was a science teacher who did not know how to wire up a plug. "Right, before we start, who knows how to wire up a plug?" Several hands went up and I carefully watched as a 13 year old expertly carried out the complex task.

In 1966 corporal punishment was still alive and well in Scottish schools and, like all young teachers of the time, I started my career with a leather belt purchased from Lochgelly in Fife. Given my own experiences at Holy Cross Academy I was no fan of using the belt but I was a fan of having control in the classroom and to achieve that you were expected to wield the Lochgelly. I used it very sparingly and did not enjoy inflicting pain on children. But I did use it; and on occasion with some force particularly when the boy standing in front of me had been guilty of bullying. As the years went by I used it less and less and strongly supported its ban in the late seventies.

At lunchtimes many of the younger staff used to have lunch in the science staff base and I remember when one of them brought in a new LP that we had to listen to. It was the Beatles "Sergeant Pepper" which took pop music to a different level and made me a fan for life.

As my first year in teaching progressed I became unsettled at St David's. The principal teacher in the chemistry department was John McGovern who was close to being the perfect boss. He was immensely likeable, helpful and encouraging but he was not able to give me a Higher Chemistry class and being the youngest in the department there was little likelihood of my getting such a class in the foreseeable future. The situation was not helped by the fact that each year there was only one Higher Chemistry class. Remember my ambition was to be a principal teacher of chemistry and if this ambition was to be fulfilled it was essential that I gained experience of Higher Chemistry. I was also uneasy that St David's was a Catholic school. I was still a practising Catholic but was starting to worry about spending my whole teaching career in Catholic schools. I was keen to widen my experience and see what life was like in a school that did not indoctrinate the children every morning with prayers and the catechism.

But probably the main reason for my itchy feet was that the school team I was running was rubbish and was getting beat most Saturdays. One of the attractions of teaching was that I would be able to run a team and be a football manager. For over thirty years my Saturdays were to have the same shape: up early to the playing fields to run my school team (often this included refereeing) and then in the car to play or manage in the afternoon. Frequently I would fall asleep when out with friends at night. I never doubted that I would be good at football management but my St David's fourteen year-olds were getting beat most weeks. It could not be my fault. The only solution was to change schools and find another team to manage and so I applied for jobs at non-denominational schools in Edinburgh.

One afternoon, Mr MacMillan, the headteacher of the school appeared at the door of my classroom and asked if he could have a word with me. I joined him in the corridor where he told me that it had come to his notice that, not only was I applying for positions at other schools but that, to make matters worse, some of these schools were not Catholic schools. I explained to him that I was keen to teach Higher Chemistry. This he understood but he was at a complete loss to understand how I could possibly be contemplating working in a Protestant school. Did I have any idea what Protestant schools were like? He then described in some detail how dreadful these establishments were. I explained that I was prepared to take my chances and he took his leave decidedly less than gruntled.

Dr Kay, the headteacher of Forrester High School in the west of Edinburgh, asked me to attend for interview. He was particularly interested in how I kept good discipline and I must have answered his questions satisfactorily because he offered me a job with the assurance that I would have a Higher Chemistry class. I left St David's at the end of June 1967 looking forward to starting at Forrester in August after the summer holidays.

Football season 1966/67 was an enjoyable one for me. Willie MacFarlane had put together a good Hawick team and playing at a lower level meant that I was able to shine. Most of the players lived in Edinburgh and so we trained two nights a week in the capital. We had two outstanding players - Andy Bowman and Malcolm Bogie. Andy was at the end of his career having played for Hearts and several other clubs south of the border. He was an old fashioned wing-half in that he was tough, secure in possession and a wonderful passer of the ball. His son David played for Hearts, Coventry City Dundee United and Scotland and had the same passion for the game as his dad. Malcolm signed for the Hibs as a fifteen year old and was at Easter Road for eight years before trying his luck in England. In 1966 he was back home, aged 26, working as an electrician in Leith's Brown Brothers and for some strange reason playing in the East of Scotland league for Hawick Royal Albert. He was the star of the team and it was obvious that he should have been playing at a higher level. What kept him back was a lack of confidence and self belief but at Hawick he was the best player in the team and he flourished and was a prolific scorer. We became great pals and I consider myself lucky to have had him in my life for so long. He is the most generous, kind, good-natured person I have ever met and to top it all is extremely handsome. He is now long retired but is gainfully employed using his lollipop to ensure that the children of Flora Stevenson's school come to no harm when crossing the road.

Towards the end of season I started to feel unsettled because I felt that I should be playing at a higher level - but there was there was little chance of getting back into Scottish league football. Instead of moving up as I had hoped I went the other way. The junior team Bonnyrigg Rose offered me a large sum of money to join them and so I signed for them at the start of the 1967/68 season just as I was starting my new job at Forrester High School. I played as badly at Bonnyrigg as I had done at Raith Rovers and this time I could not blame the manager because Bill Durie, who ran the team, was a great person as was his coach Andy Kelly. I was seeing Willie MacFarlane socially and hearing how well Hawick were doing in my absence and I longed to be back where I had played well. The only good thing about playing for Bonnyrigg was that, since it is just outside Edinburgh, I was able to take my mother, Wee Bridget, to all the home games. She was not concerned about how well I played; she just wanted to be with me. After three months I gave back all of my signing-on money, was released from my contract and re-signed for Hawick. Events were to show that this was a wise decision because at the end of the season Willie MacFarlane was appointed manager of Stirling Albion and took me to Stirling with him along with Walter Lowry, George Brough, Steve Sherry, Jimmy Logan and Billy Armstrong. Malcolm Bogie missed out because he suffered a leg break towards the end of season.

Forrester High School

I started at Forrester in August 1967 at the same time as I commenced a new season playing for Bonnyrigg Rose. When I walked into the science staff base I met a strange looking, slightly familiar little chap who immediately asked me, " Are you wee Christie who played for Edinburgh schools?" I affirmed that I was and he introduced himself as John Irvine, head of biology, and one of the selectors for the Edinburgh secondary schools team. He then asked me if I wanted to run a school team and was delighted when I agreed to do so. I was less than delighted on hearing that I would be in charge of the third year team who were hopeless. For the next three years John Irvine ("Charlie" to the pupils) was very much a mentor to me. He was devoted to the kids who loved and respected him and I was determined to try to be like him although I was much less easy-going than him and a good bit stricter with the pupils.

My principal teacher of chemistry, Jimmy Auld, was also a big influence on me but in a different way; he was an expert in his subject and a terrific teacher and I strived to be as knowledgeable and assured as he was. One of my colleagues in the chemistry department also made a big impression on me; I had been at university with Gladys Corbett but she had been teaching a year longer than me and was much more experienced than me. She was a slip of a girl, very pretty, and a great teacher. As with all good teachers it seemed effortless for her and I marvelled how she could command a class without seeming to do much and never needing to raise her voice. I thought she was wonderful. John Irvine, Jimmy Auld and Gladys Corbett were professional, with a pride in their work and all three had a great relationship with their pupils; I could not have had better role models.

I was given the Higher class I longed for and I quickly settled into life at Forrester. The school is situated in west Edinburgh beside the Broomhouse housing scheme with the Sighthill scheme just to the south and middle-class Corstophine to the north. Back then the youngsters from all three districts attended Forrester and so it was a large school catering for pupils with a wide range of abilities. I joke that these were my halcyon days when I used to get paid for belting "Proddies" and that, when I got home, my mother would ask, "How many the day son?" and if she was pleased with my answer I got an extra tattie. The truth was that I seldom used the "Lochgelly".

Then, in April 1968 my life changed and not for the better. It was the Edinburgh Spring Holiday Monday and so I had a day off and was practising with my ball in Holyrood Park. Our bedroom window, which overlooked the park opened, and there was Margaret frantically beckoning for me to come home. I raced back to the house and she told me that the shopkeeper at the corner had told her that my mother had phoned to say that my dad was ill (we did not have a telephone). I sprinted the mile or so to Loganlea Drive and raced up the stairs. Wee Bridget was at the door crying uncontrollably. She told me that my dad had a heart attack and that an ambulance was on the way. I went into the bedroom and my dad told me that he had a terrific pain in his chest and down his arm. I had no idea what to do. After a couple of minutes he started to have a massive heart attack. I was powerless to do anything but remember with great guilt that I thought "Please die dad"; I just wanted his pain to stop. After a few seconds all was quiet and I knew he was dead. The ambulance men soon arrived and confirmed this. I was 25 and at that moment my youth ended.

My mother was inconsolable but I had to think how was I going to tell my brother, Peter, who was at Clermiston managing Jock's Lodge Thistle - his pub team. Clermiston is on the other side of Edinburgh and I had no car. Margaret's mother, Molly, came to the rescue and let me borrow her's. I arrived at the football pitches and asked Peter's brother-in-law, Charlie Marrins, to bring Peter to the car. Telling my brother that our 56 year old father had died was the most difficult thing I have done in life. I am now in my seventies and I still cry when I think about it.

My father died during Holy Week which precedes Easter Sunday and, as a result, there could be no requiem mass and his body was not even allowed into the church. There was a short service for him in the Co-op's funeral parlour. Life changing decisions should not be made as a result of a single event that was mishandled, but the hurt caused to my mother by this dreadful example of Catholic bureaucracy caused me to seriously examine my faith, which was also dealt a blow by the fact that the priest designated to comfort the family was intellectually challenged. He gave my mother no support and having to deal with him strengthened my belief that the Church would ordinate anybody who was prepared to be celibate and could just about master enough Latin to conduct mass. My faith was already getting a bit shaky and my dad's death sounded its death knell. I have never attended mass since April 1968 and I am now an atheist although I still do believe that the Catholic Church is an instrument for good.

My dad was buried on a Friday and I played for Hawick Royal Albert on the Saturday. I never considered not playing, believing that there is little purpose in suspending normal life because of a death. Wee Bridget came with me in the team bus and Margaret's mother, Molly, was with her to lend support. We won comfortably and that night Bridget slept with Margaret and me in the only bed in our small flat.

My mother then had to face the reality that she now had to earn a living. The income from her school cleaning and her various other cleaning jobs was not enough to keep her. Her friend, Jean Rogan, had a part-time job as a barmaid in Princes Street's Mount Royal Hotel and Jean used her influence to get Bridget a full-time position serving behind the bar. She was only 53 and for the next 30 or so years my mother worked as a barmaid and loved the job because it gave her the chance to do what she loved most - meeting people and have a blether!

At the start of my second year at Forrester in August 1968 (I was now playing for Stirling Albion) my principal teacher, Jimmy Auld, was given a one year leave of absence to study for a masters degree at East Anglia university. The headteacher, Dr Kay, called me into his office and asked me if I would become acting principal teacher of chemistry for the year that Jimmy would be gone. I jumped at the chance and at the age of 25 I was in charge of a department in a large school with six or so older and much more experienced teachers to manage. Dr Kay had obviously taken a shine to me and it was a lucky career break for me.

The first whole school principal teachers' meeting I attended, however, did not go well. The chemistry staff gave me lots of ideas of things I should bring up at the meeting and I left the science staff-base nervous but full of determination that I was going to make my presence felt. Dr Kay was off ill and the depute, Jim Mitchell, was chairing the meeting. The first item on the agenda was the arrangements for Dr Kay's retiral dinner. One of the older PT's rose to his feet and stated that I had no right to be there and that I should leave the meeting. One or two of the younger PT's spoke on my behalf but the matter went to a vote and there was a clear majority in favouring of throwing me out. And so I left, tail between legs, trying to hold back the tears! When I returned to the science staff base a couple of female teachers cuddled me and told me not to worry.

I did not worry; I went to war with the old guard. I still had the job of writing report cards for my register class.

The very experienced principal teacher of technical education sent me the marks in an incorrect format. I sent them back to him and would not give in when he came to see me and started shouting that I was an "upstart". I refused to lend the chemistry department's film projector to the head of geography even though he had arranged to use it for showing films (porn) at his rugby club. He was a tall lad and had been a terrific rugby player when younger. As he picked me up in the corridor and drew his fist back my resolve weakened but he relented and left, telling me that I was a "wee prick". I was also even more voluble in defending football in the rugby orientated all male staffroom.

Dr Kay returned and, to my delight, at the next principal teachers' meeting made it clear that he was angry at my ejection and that I had as much right to be there as any of them. I then started building bridges and before too long was very friendly with just about all the principal teachers especially, Jim Lacey, the frightening head of geography. Crying together into our beer seemed to work for both of us.

I was thrown into management at the deep-end but I enjoyed it from the start. Management in schools is about making sure the kids are looked after and receive the best possible education and also helping the teachers to give their best. The above is an over simplification but I have never had any doubts about what my job was as a manager in a school. Often you have to be the referee when things go wrong between pupil and teacher. My attitude was that you always did what was right; the skill was in making sure that the pupil and the teacher felt that they had been dealt with fairly. Sounds easy, but having to tell a much older and more experienced teacher that they had messed up was difficult and I used to be close to hyperventilation before such meetings. I have a low tolerance level with regard to poor practices and it is in my nature to try and improve things. When you are looking after children, sweeping things under the carpet is never an option but also looking for problems is generally not a good idea.

After a year Jimmy Auld returned and I reverted to being an ordinary teacher although I was made a "Special Assistant" which meant that I earned slightly more for taking on a few non-onerous duties. Then I got another lucky break - Jimmy Auld left to take up a lecturer's post in education at the newly created Dundee University. His job was advertised and I applied.

At that time the change to comprehensive secondary schools was in full swing. Three-year junior secondary schools were being closed and their pupils moved to comprehensive schools. Just east of Forrester, at Stenhouse, was Carrickvale Junior Secondary School, which was to close with all its pupils going to Forrester. All the promoted posts would be filled by Forrester teachers with the Carrickvale teachers being absorbed by Forrester on conserved salaries. The principal teacher of chemistry at Carrickvale, Greg Purves, applied for the vacancy at Forrester and my chances of being appointed did not look too great since Greg was much older than me, vastly more experienced and good at his job. At the interview Councillor Knox asked me why, as a former dux of Holy Cross Academy, I did not get a first class honours degree. I answered lamely omitting to mention that a lot of my time had been taken up with professional football. Well, I did get the job and Greg Purves was now working for me; fortunately he was wonderfully supportive and a real gentleman. He taught me a lesson in how to handle disappointment. After a few months he moved to a principal teacher job in another school.

I was 27, running the chemistry department in a large school and playing for Stirling Albion and life was great. I should also mention that I was a father. On 18th September 1968 Margaret gave birth to our son Kevan; the funny spelling is because Derek Kevan was scoring goals for West Bromwich at the time. Kevan was born on a Wednesday morning and in the evening I played for Stirling Albion against Stranraer; and so I played football the day after my dad was buried and also on the actual day my first child was born - very revealing.

Schools football was a huge part of my life at Forrester. When I started there in 1967 I was given the third year team to run but they got beat every week. John Irvine kept encouraging me by telling me that the following year I would have the first year team and that primary school teachers had been telling him that lots of good players were coming up to Forrester. I was leaving nothing to chance and, in the summer of '68, I visited all the primaries to let those coming to Forrester know that trials for the Forrester football team started immediately; and so in May and June I was training 11 and 12 year-old boys for a football season that did not start until August. I ran that team for four years and had great success and many of those boys became good friends of mine. I have fond memories of: David Anderson, Kenny Sinclair, Dougie Aikman, David Scobie, Ian Dumayne, Terence Laird, Davie Dick, Peter Jenkinson, Peter Keddie, Willie Prior, Ally McLeod and many others. The star of the team was Tom Hendrie who left school to play for Dundee and then played for me for 12 years at Meadowbank Thistle and later managed St Mirren in the Premier League. Tom was one of the most talented players I ever managed and over many years I had great pleasure watching him play. He is now not far off sixty years old and is one of my closest friends.

In the year below these lads there was a left back that I drafted into my team for the big matches and who went on to play 485 games for Manchester United; his name is Arthur Albiston.

A couple of other pupils are memorable for reasons other than football. Les McKeown was a handful as regards discipline but I did notice that he seemed unusually popular with the girls - not as popular as he became when he was lead singer in the Bay City Rollers. There was also a lovely girl called Lesley Wearmonth who is now Mrs Bernard Gallacher (Ryder Cup captain) and mother of Sky Sports' Kirsty.

The death of my dad had hit me hard and two years later I was again grieving. John Irvine had become much more of than just a colleague; he was a great man who was loved by his pupils and respected by all those who considered their job to be about more than classroom teaching but also entailed looking after and caring for your pupils. He started to complain about headaches and a few weeks later told me that he had a brain tumour. I was with him just before he died and the whole experience affected me deeply; I was ill for a few days and that feeling of sadness I had experienced when my dad passed away returned and stayed with me for months.

But generally I had a happy time at Forrester. When there is a small age gap between you and your pupils they can relate easily to you and they become more like friends. Some memories:

- I was training my school team and was playing football with them in a game that became a little competitive - I was 26 and the boys were 14. I tackled a thin little lad (forgotten his name) and our shins clashed. It was an accident but my legs are like tree trunks; the unfortunate victim's were of the twig variety. He was in distress and I decided to take him to accident and emergency and instructed one of the boys to inform his parents. An x-ray showed a hair-line fracture and his leg was put in plaster. I drove him home and the parents were grateful for the way I had looked after him. The question was then asked,

"How did it actually happen, Mr Christie?" Overcoming my embarrassment I told them, fearing the worst. Fortunately they were very understanding but I have never forgotten the dread I felt as I was about to tell parents that I had broken their son's leg.

- A boy in the class had brought a ball to school and at the end of the lesson challenged me to a game of "keepie-uppie" which involved heading the ball against the classroom wall. He went first - not bad, but I was confident I could beat him. It was going well with all the class counting out-loud when in walked Dick Barr, the science adviser for the City of Edinburgh. Fortunately he saw the funny side of it and went on to explain that he was doing development work for the government of Botswana and had been asked to find them a science adviser and he thought that I was the man for the job. I new nothing of Botswana and the thought of moving to deepest Africa terrified me and so I passed on that one.

- It was a lovely summer's afternoon and I was showing the class how to make bromine gas. A little of the gas leaked and there was a strong bleach type smell in the classroom. For the safety of the kids I took them out to the playing fields and it happened that a ball was handy so we had a game of football and then we had races because some of the class thought they could run faster than me. Next time that class came to chemistry it was again a lovely June afternoon and I gave in to their pleas to again make bromine. Once again we were out in the playing fields. Next day the depute headteacher, Bob Sutherland, called me to his office and said that several teachers had expressed surprise that football seemed a mandatory part of the chemistry syllabus and that life was being made difficult for them as their pupils were demanding to be taken outside. Reluctantly I agreed to a cessation in the manufacturing of bromine.

At the start of the 1970's secondary education in Scotland was expanding rapidly and more was being expected of schools. In an attempt to meet these expectations a new management post was created to fill the gap between principal teacher and depute headteacher. These new positions were to be called assistant headteachers and suddenly my life depended upon being an assistant headteacher. I had entered teaching with my sights set on being a principal teacher of chemistry and had achieved this goal at the age of 27 and now I wanted to do more. I wanted to stretch myself and when I looked at those in the very senior positions I thought, "I can do that". The thought of having more power also appealed to me.

And so I started to apply for the new assistant headteacher posts. I remember being interviewed at Liberton High School by their respected and erudite headteacher, Henry Philip, who asked me what had I been reading. I was about to answer "the back pages of the 'Daily Record'" until I realised that he was referring to books on education theory. "Nothing" I said and I could see from his expression that he was less than impressed by my answer. Not surprisingly I did not get that job but I did hone up on current education theory and was better prepared for subsequent interviews. I then managed to get on the short leet for a post at Firhill High School. I felt I did well and was disappointed when the director of education informed me that I had missed out but there was good news; the committee liked me and had put me on the short leet for an assistant headteacher post at Portobello High School and I was instructed to attend for a preliminary interview with the headteacher, Jack Baggaley. That interview was not encouraging because Mr Baggaley told me that he had read my application form but he felt that, as I was only 30, I was far too young to be an assistant headteacher at what was then Scotland's largest school with a roll of about 2,500.

The next day I appeared for interview before the esteemed members of Edinburgh Council's Education Committee's "Appointments Sub-Committee" and was appointed assistant headteacher at Portobello High School in spite of Mr Baggaley's lack of enthusiasm.

Before leaving Forrester I had to give a conducted tour of the school to those who had applied for my post. I got on particularly well with one tall applicant who was a bit fierce looking but was by far the best candidate. Back in our all-male staffroom my colleagues were pumping me with questions about him. I had no idea what all the fuss was about until it was explained to me that he was Jim Telfer, one of Scotland's greatest rugby players - he got the job. I was sad to leave Forrester but excited at the new challenges that faced me at Portobello High School.

Stirling Albion

I joined Stirling in August 1968 just as I took up the temporary principal teacher post at Forrester. I was now 25 and I saw this as my last chance to play regular Scottish league football. At Hawick Royal Albert things had been terrific - we were the best team in the East of Scotland League, I was playing well and I enjoyed a great relationship with the manager, Willie MacFarlane. In the summer of 1967 Margaret and I had gone with Willie and his wife, Joyce, and their two kids, Ian and Jacqueline, on a hugely enjoyable driving holiday to Spain. Because of our close friendship Willie would ask my advice on team selection and tactics but all of this was to change.

Although I yearned to play in midfield I was still looked on as a winger and at Stirling there were two wingers better than me - Billy Armstrong on the left and Mattie McPhee on the right. Billy was a powerful runner and a great crosser while Mattie had real pace and was a regular scorer. I pleaded with Willie to play me in midfield, and occasionally he did, but for much of the time I was selected only when Billy or Mattie were injured or had a dip in form. Experience has taught me that footballers are not the most objective when evaluating themselves and I was no different. I felt I should be playing in midfield every week and I was not shy in expressing this view to Willie.

My advice on team matters was also being asked less often. An old friend of Willie's, Johnny Mochan, had been appointed assistant manager and he and I were not bosom buddies. Willie started to listen more to Johnny and less to me; my nose was firmly out of joint. The friction at the football club resulted in Willie and I seeing each other less often socially although we would still have nights-out with Malcolm Bogie and his wife Margaret.

In those days there was only two divisions in Scottish football and Stirling had just been relegated from the top league, the First Division, and had a good team. Star of the team was young Henry Hall who was a super little player as well as being a great lad. But Willie was finding the step up to a higher league difficult; the players were often not sure of what tactical formation we were playing and on occasion I would speak up and have a public row with Willie and Johnny Mochan, both of whom I thought did not have a clue about organising a team.

We had one trip to the Forfar when Willie gave us our team-talk on the bus and left the players totally confused as to the tactics we were employing. I tried to help him but was shouted down. At the start of the season Henry Hall had made a comment to Willie that he did not look forward to playing on the small pitches that are common in the Second Division. It was now three months into the season and Henry was tearing opposition defences apart but, the Forfar pitch was small, and so he was dropped. We were comprehensively defeated and in the post mortem a few days later there was mayhem as the players voiced their opinions about the lack of tactical clarity and I will always remember Wee Henry asking Willie, "How can you have dropped me because of a passing comment I made three months ago in the close season?". Half-way through the season Willie spoke to me and said that St Johnstone had made a good offer for Henry and that he was thinking of accepting it. I was against the idea and stressed to him that without Henry promotion was going to be difficult. Henry was transferred to St Johnstone where he was a huge success.

Even without Henry the team did well and, as the season progressed, we were just behind Mothewell at the top of the league and were strong challengers for promotion. We then went to Stenhousemuir, whom in those days Stirling Albion always beat. One of the strengths of the side was our centre-forward, Joe Hughes, who was brave and a regular scorer. Willie read out the team and Joe Hughes was playing in defence at left back, a position he seemingly had played when much younger. We were a shambles and were well beaten. Next week Joe was back at centre-forward. Many times later I asked Willie why he had played Joe at left back without getting an answer that made sense.

Willie was great at making you laugh and he fancied himself as an entertainer - he was also a good singer. A friend of his had been over in the United States and had brought back a record of a nightclub comedian. Willie was always playing the record and had perfected his New Jersey accent. At Stirling Albion's annual dinner the directors and their wives were sitting at the top table - all of them affluent pillars of society. Willie

decided to entertain the company and launched into the 'gags' from the record. Gauging the audience was not one of his strengths and I remember the one that went down least well:
"This sailor has been on the ocean for three months and when he comes home he goes straight to the brothel. He is enjoying the services of the lady of the night and asks her, "How am I doing?" She replies, "You're doing three knots". "What do you mean I am doing three knots?" "You're not in, you're not hard, and you're not getting you're money back!" All of those at the top table walked out.

Our promotion hopes stayed alive until the second last game of the season when we were defeated on a miserable Wednesday night at Stranraer. I played on the wing and did not do well and reacted badly to the criticism I received from Willie.

The last game of the season was at Motherwell who had already won the league. Before he announced the team Willie told the players that after the match he would let each individual know whether or not they were being retained for the following season. I was not selected and watched the match from the stand feeling that I was definitely about to be released. The game finished (a defeat) and all 20 or so players were sitting in the away changing room waiting to find out their future. Willie was outside in the corridor and he would open the changing room door and call out the name of the player he wanted to see next. Eventually my turn came and I went through the door fearing the worst. Suddenly I felt a massive sense of relief because there was Willie, hand outstretched, with a big smile on his face. I took his hand and he said, "Goodbye" looking very pleased with himself. I felt numb inside and, without uttering a word, I returned to the dressing room, desolate, said farewell to my erstwhile teammates, and went home with the realisation that Scottish league football was over for me.

That incident was a lesson to me in how not to give people bad news. In the years that lay ahead I would have to do so on many occasions and I came to the realisation that there is no easy way; but I was never as unfeeling and smart-arsed as Willie had been on that day.

The East of Scotland League season had not yet finished and Frank Duncan, who had played in goal for Motherwell, asked me to turn out for Gala Fairydean whom he was managing. I loved playing and so I agreed to do so. I played about six matches for Gala and thoroughly enjoyed it. One of my teammates was a young lad from Wallyford whom Hearts had loaned to Gala so that he could get experience. Jim Jeffries went on to have a long and successful career in football as a player and manager.

Less than a couple of months after being freed by Stirling Albion my doorbell rang and standing on the doorstep, looking slightly embarrassed, was Willie MacFarlane. He said that he had made a mistake in letting me go and asked if I would come back. Cutting your nose off to spite your face has never been an option for me and I knew that I was not going to get a better club and so I readily agreed to return, provided that I got a chance to play in midfield. Willie assured me that my days as a winger were over and so I signed for a second time for Stirling Albion delighted that I was getting another chance. There was also an improvement in my relationship with Willie, although never again were we as close as in our time together at Hawick Royal Albert.

At the start of the 1969/70 season I was playing regularly in centre midfield and was thoroughly enjoying it. Playing behind me at left-back was a very raw but wonderfully committed youngster, Erich Schaedler. A couple of months into the season Willie asked me to stay behind after training because he wanted to have a chat. He then told me that he was about to become manager of Hibs. Bob Shankly had resigned and Willie's friend and ex-teammate at Easter Road, Tommy Younger, was now a director at the club and he had asked Willie to be the new manager. I was astounded but pleased for Willie who had a huge affection for Hibs and a massive enthusiasm for football. Not surprisingly his first signing was Erich Schaedler who went on to become part of Willie Ormond's Scotland squad in the 1974 world cup. Erich died tragically aged 36 and it was sad that such a good person was so troubled that he took his own life.

Willie's successor as manager was Frank Joyner who had played for Raith Rovers, Sheffield United and Dundee. His football career had been interrupted by the

Second World War in which he served with distinction rising to the rank of captain and at one time operated behind German lines. He was tall and handsome with dark wavy hair and was charming, affable and very much the gentleman - you could not help but like him. Unfortunately he had little idea of the tactical side of the game and as a manager was in the "too nice" category; one Thursday night he cut training short so that we could get home in time to see the "Miss World" competition.

Back then football was changing tactically and by the time Frank became manager all teams had adopted the twin centre-half formation. Frank had been brought up in the days of a single centre-half and two wing-halfs and he was not at all keen on the new fangled defensive system. In a match at Clydebank he selected a team with five forwards and only one centre-back. The opposition could not cope with our all out attack and at half-time we were 4-0 up. In the second half they took advantage of the fact that their twin strikers were facing only one centre-half and we were defeated 6-5. After the match Frank told us it had been a great game and that he had thoroughly enjoyed it - but he never repeated that experiment.

That season we finished a respectable fourth but did not do well the following season and towards the end of 1970 Frank was sacked. A replacement was not immediately appointed and for a while the team was run by coach Walter Roy ably assisted by the goal-keeping coach Tom McLaren. I travelled to training with

Walter who was Principal Teacher of Physical Education at Musselburgh Grammar School and Tom and I had played together at Hawick and were both mad keen Hibs supporters - I was therefore "well in" with those in charge.

During the interregnum we had a great result defeating Motherwell in the Scottish Cup. That was no mean feat because a few days before the match the "Well" had beaten mighty Tottenham Hotspur in the Texaco Cup. I played in midfield against a young Tom Forsyth who went on to a wonderful career with Rangers and Scotland and at centre-forward they had Dixie Deans of Celtic fame. In the round following we were defeated by Dundee who were still a force in Scottish football. Our cause was not helped by one of our players, Kenny Dowds, being sent off in the first-half. Kenny had played in the Berwick Rangers team that famously knocked Rangers out of the Scottish Cup in 1967. He was a good player and a likeable lad who, after football, lost his way and died at the age of 50.

Eventually a new manager was appointed and to my delight it was my former manager at Dundee, Bob Shankly, who had been tempted out of retirement. He was now 60 years old and had given up management after a reasonably successful period with Hibs. Age had, however, not blunted his enthusiasm and I detected little difference in him. On his first night at training I was receiving treatment for a slight knock; seeing me on the treatment table his greeting to me was, "Come on

Terry, even good players cannae afford to miss training".

Under Bob's management we immediately became a proper team and, although we never achieved it, were continually challenging for promotion to Scotland's top division. I knew that Bob wanted you to work hard and apply yourself and that is exactly what I did and so I was normally in the team.
However, we did have our moments. I was now playing in centre midfield but, having been a winger, I liked to wander out wide. If you are not the nominated winger, opponents do not expect you to take them on down the line and are surprised when you do so. During the first half of a match against Queen of the South at Palmerston Park I had been thoroughly enjoying myself getting wide on the left, taking on the right back and putting in crosses - I thought I was playing really well. During the half-time break, with the score 0-0, Bob made it clear that he did not share this view. "Terry, you are a midfielder and not a fucking winger. I expect you to sit in the midfield and no to be running oot to the wing all the fucking time." I had never spoke back to him but this time I did - big mistake! " You're no telling me that Alan Ball (a member of England's 1966 world cup winning team) just sits in the midfield and disnae get wide." Bob then went wild, "Alan Ball, Alan fucking Ball, you're no comparing yourself with Alan Ball. I've fucking heard everything now. You go out and sit in midfield as you are supposed to do and do not let me hear another word about fucking Alan Ball." My gas at a severe peep I said nothing and went out for the second-

half, in the huff, but wise enough to know that I had better do as told. We won the match 2-0 and Bob was pleased and happy and ready to forgive. I was relieved when he said, "That was much better, Terry." My teammates, however, loved to remind me of the night I compared myself to Alan Ball!

A couple of other matches have stayed fresh in my memory. 1973 was the year Leeds United gave the great Billy Bremner a testimonial. He was a Stirling lad and it was his ambition to play against the Albion and so manager Don Revie took his team of stars to Stirling to play us at Annfield. I was a substitute for the match but got on for the last 25 minutes and actually tackled Bremner and was threatened by him; I felt a real player! I also remember playing at Parkhead against a good Celtic side. Mickey Lawson was playing for us as a striker in the left channel and I was in midfield behind him. He was having to spend the bulk of the game checking back on their young right-back, who was driving forward at every opportunity. If we were to get a goal we needed Mickey up the park and I shouted to him to stay in a forward position and ignore the right-back; my actual words were, "Just leave him, he cannae play." The youngster was Danny McGrain - Scotland's best ever right-back. My player assessment improved with time!

Bob Shankly was sparing with praise and it was unusual for him to single out any individual. One day after narrowly winning a match he said in the dressing room, "That was poor - thank fuck we had Terry" I had never before been praised by him and I was as pleased as it was possible to be. I have always remembered how happy I was that day and I never forgot how powerful praise can be in making someone feel good about themselves. It also struck home with me that Bob should have praised his players more than he did. As a manager I was careful not to cheapen praise by overuse but also to say "well done" to individuals when it was deserved.

At the end of the 1972-73 season in which we narrowly missed promotion Bob Shankly decided to become general manager and he appointed Frank Beattie as manager. I was now 30 years old and was not playing as regularly in the team mainly because of the talent of youngsters like Rab Duffin and Jim Clark. The competition for midfield places had been increased also by the signing from Morton of John Murphy who had played for Hibs and, like me, was from Edinburgh. Mickey Lawson was also from Edinburgh and John, Mickey and I became great friends and still are. I see both of them every week and I am hugely lucky to have them as my friends. John was out of work having gone from full-time with Morton to part-time with Stirling Albion. Through a friend of mine I arranged for him to have an interview with the civil service. He got the job and spent the next 40 years in the civil service; I never tire of telling him that he has me to thank for his "gold-plated" pension. Another dear friend from my Stirling days is the sprinter and raconteur George McNeill whom I see regulary and whose company is a delight.

With Frank Beattie as manager I played fewer and fewer first team matches and it was no surprise to me when, at the end of the 1973-74 season, I was not offered a contract. I played 142 games for Stirling and I loved my time there. In playing regularly in Scotland's second league I felt I had made the most of my ability. I look back with great affection on my teammates in those days and I learned about the massive dedication that is required to hold down a demanding full-time job whilst playing part-time football at a decent level. I never forgot this and, as a manager, always had realistic expectations from my players as they tried to balance the demands of two jobs.

It was now time for me to become a football manager and in preparation I had taken time out of two summer holidays to go to England and become a fully qualified Football Association coach. I had been 14 years as a professional footballer and had been managed mainly by: Bob Shankly; George Farm; Willie MacFarlane; Frank Joyner; and Frank Beattie. From Willie MacFarlane I learned the importance of enthusiasm and humour and having players who are athletic. But the man who taught me most was Bob Shankly; he showed me that the manager must have the respect of the players and that he must set an example in the way he conducts himself. From the others I learned what not to do.

Portobello High School

In the first week of May in 1973 I started at Portobello High School in the newly created post of assistant headteacher. I was playing for Stirling Albion and by now had two little boys. Our second son was born on 7th November 1971 and, as with the first born I was tasked, with finding a name for him. Martin Peters was playing great for West Ham and England and so, for no other reason, the newly born became Martin. I immediately hated the name, which did not suit him. When he was about six he joined his big brother, Kevan, at Portobello Thistle football club and one of the kids there starting to call him Max, which he loved and I loved and he therefore became Max. His mum Margaret preferred Martin but eventually she had to admit defeat and accept that she had a son called Max. We had also moved into a new house - a semi-detached villa in the Mountcastle district not far from Portobello High School.

On my first day at Portobello I entered the school with a new suit and scrubbed face about 20 minutes before any staff had arrived and was shown by a janitor into the staffroom. Although I was 30 I looked much younger and was in a state of high agitation. After a while a young teacher about my age came in, introduced himself as Colin Bryce and told me taught art. He then enquired what I was doing there. I answered, "Assistant head". "What's your subject?", he asked. "Chemistry", I replied. "But the chemistry department already has an assistant principal teacher" he said obviously nonplussed. To his amazement and my embarrassment I explained that I was to be assistant head for the whole school. He apologised profusely and a good friendship formed that day - years later Colin became a professor at Napier University.

Eventually I was ushered in to see the headteacher Mr Jack Baggaley, who was even less enthusiastic to see me than he had been at my pre-appointment interview. He made it clear that I was not his choice but that, now that I was there, I was to take my time to get to know the school. As an assistant headteacher I would teach half a chemistry timetable and would spend the rest of my time on whole school management tasks. The only problem was that the only management task Mr Baggaley had for me was to coordinate outdoor education in the school. Now, I was a city boy with next to no interest in the countryside and the only hill I had ever climbed was Edinburgh's Arthur Seat. There was nobody in the world of education less suited for the job of outdoor education coordinator than me! At the interview Mr Baggaley made it clear also that all the senior staff in the school wore academic gowns and that he expected me to do likewise. And so I bought an academic gown and wore it for over a year until I was eventually confident enough to refuse to wear it. Years later an ex-pupil frequently took delight in telling me that, "you used to prance about the school in an academic gown fancying yourself".

The school had six senior staff: the headteacher; two depute heads (Isabel Wishart and Derek McIvor); and three assistant heads (Ken Anderson, Margaret Reid and me.) The two deputes were in a continuous power struggle and had cornered all the main administrative jobs and were not relinquishing any power to a wet-behind-the-years-youngster. I had so much free time that I used to take a book to school to read in my office.

One thing I did learn during a difficult first year was to bite my tongue and not fall out with those more senior than me. A piece of advice I have often given is that if you wish your career to advance the second worse thing you can do is argue with your boss - the worst thing is winning the argument. I was not about to make that mistake but it was difficult at senior management meetings when there was no agenda and it was frowned upon if you raised a question about the management of the school. On one occasion frustration got the better of me and I issued to all the senior management team my suggestions for improvement in some aspect of the school organisation. The paper was dismissed out of hand and Miss Wishart got a hold of me and told me that issuing papers was not a good idea as it only upset people; she did not add, "especially me".

During that time I did go on a lot of courses - Mr Baggaley was good at finding courses for me to go on. I remember spending a week at Catterick Camp learning about the army and another week in South Wales at Atlantic College, an international residential sixth form college. During my week there I listened to a concert by the pianist Arthur Rubenstein and was introduced to Harry Secombe of Goons fame. The City of Edinburgh was granting one scholarship per year to one of its pupils and the idea was that I would be able to advise such a pupil. None of the pupils at Portobello ever applied - but it was still a memorable week and I also took the chance to see Cardiff City play York City!

Gradually things got better. Jack Baggaley was a decent man who had been a major during the war with the Chindits in Burma and was involved in fighting the Japanese at close quarters. I started to get on well with him and with all the other members of the management team. Isabel Wishart would delegate jobs to me and Derek McIvor took time and trouble to explain the intricacies of the school timetable.

Things changed when two new assistant headteachers were appointed and shared my large office with me. Norrie Brown was an expert in learning support and never backed away from a fight and the other newcomer was Jim Telfer, who had succeeded me as Principal Teacher of Chemistry at Forrester. Together we became the "new guard" and worked jointly to bring about change and make the school more efficient so that it provided a better deal for the pupils. Jim is one of the most memorable characters I have ever met and in the three or so years we worked together I grew fond of him. He had finished playing by then and was managing his local team Melrose. His enthusiasm for rugby new no bounds and I learned much from him about the complexities of that game. I remember sharing his disappointment when he was unsuccessful in his first attempt to become the coach of our national team.

Eventually he did coach Scotland and the British Lions with great success. He is always portrayed as a hard taskmaster but I was able to see a gentler side of him in the way he spoke to and cared for children. But he was a strict disciplinarian and after giving a youngster a dressing down he would always finish with the question, "Do you understand?". This forced the pupil to respond and was very effective; these were words I used frequently in later years.

One way to get ahead is to have an essential technical skill; if you are one of the few people in the organisation to have this essential skill then you have an edge. In the management of a large school the essential skill worth requiring is that of school timetabling. The timetable gives reality to the curriculum and a well made timetable can greatly enhance the learning experience of the pupils. There were 40 periods in the week at Portobello High and every 40 minutes over 2000 children would get up and move to another classroom and another teacher. The problem was exacerbated by the fact that the 400 or so first year pupils were housed in an annexe down the road. I had become interested in whole school timetabling at Forrester and had been lucky enough to have been sent on a course for it by the Deputy Head, Bob Sutherland. I loved the logic of timetabling and trying to solve the many problems it threw up.

At Portobello after second year, for timetabling purposes, the pupils were separated into two groups - those studying a modern language and those not taking a language. These groups were offered different course choices and except for English and Mathematics were never in the same class. It was far from ideal as the subject options for pupils were restricted and a talented youngster who was a non-linguist, was kept apart from other talented kids most of whom studied a language. I hated the system and knew it could be done better but could not persuade senior management to change the tried and trusted method.

The only way to show them that my proposed system would work was to timetable the whole school with the new system - and that is what I did. Working late at night, after football training and when the boys were in bed, I produced individual timetables for the 2,300 pupils at the school. It took me a few months but producing the prototype was hugely satisfying and, more importantly, it brought about the change I desired.

After a couple of years I no longer complained of having little to do and had settled in well as part of the management team and loved working at Portobello just as much as I had at Forrester. As part of the school's developing guidance system I became a year head with a pastoral responsibility for the 400 pupils in the year. As the 1970's progressed the use of corporal punishment in Scottish schools became less and less acceptable. More and more children were reluctant to hold their hand out so that they could be beaten with a thick piece of leather. There were about 140 teachers at Portobello and many of the older ones were finding it difficult to keep discipline with an increasing number of pupils refusing to "take the belt". Pupils in my year who refused the belt were sent to me and it was my task to beat the recalcitrant. It was a part of the job I hated as often the child had often done little wrong. My usual practice was to counsel the youngsters as to the errors of their ways and then explain to them that I was going to lightly tap them on the hand with the belt but that they had to return to the classroom blowing on their hands as if they had been severely dealt with. This system worked well and colleagues would frequently tell me that it was a mystery to them how I could get the kids to take the belt. More serious infractions usually resulted in the child being sent home and their parents called in.

I remember one twelve year old cheeky wee boy with a disadvantaged background who was belted every time he went to history because he did not have a pencil. Given all his problems the bairn kept forgetting that he had to have a pencil, but the elderly principal teacher of history was adamant that standards had to be maintained and that he expected me to do something about it. I did. I spoke to Denis (who was a menace) and told him that before he went to history he had to go into the school office in the annexe and he would be given a pencil. This he did, the belting stopped, and the principal teacher of history thought I was wonderful!

One day I had to telephone the police because a little girl had stolen a substantial amount of money from her mother, bought all her pals sweets, and then had "done a runner" with her closest friend. About eleven o'clock that night I was preparing to go to bed when the door bell rang and, when I opened the door, who should be standing there but the two little runaway girls who were frightened to go home and who thought that things would go easier for them if Mr Christie took them home. So I took them home and things did go easier for them.

Being the youngest of the management team I was usually given the job of supervising the fairly regular Friday night discos that were held in the school hall. It was a demanding job but one I enjoyed. In 1974 the Ray Stevens record "The Streak" was popular and streaking was becoming more and more common. At one of the discos a pupil, Brian Ross, whispered to me, "Sir, you had better go into the girls' cloakroom. There is a lassie going to do the streak and she is daft enough to dae it". I charged into the girls' and true enough there was a young 16 year old naked, with all her pals around her laughing. I bawled at her to get her clothes on and left the room wondering what to do about it. I returned to the cloakroom after a few minutes and to my relief she was fully dressed. I said no more, needing time to ponder whether or not I should take disciplinary action. In the end I decided to take no action influenced by the fact that she was a well behaved and hard working pupil and probably had no intention of running through the hall with no clothes on but was just having a laugh with her pals. However, whenever I passed her in the corridor I could not resist saying, "Oh hello Susan, never recognised you with your clothes on".

As I have mentioned, half my week was taken up with teaching; I taught chemistry and general science. In first and second year an integrated science course was taught and, although I had no qualification in the subject, I was required to teach biology. At that time sexual education had taken off and part of my job was to teach reproduction to the first year pupils. Like all my colleagues I faced this with trepidation. One day I was in full flow explaining how sperm left the erect penis and entered the womb where it fertilised the waiting egg. At that point a wee lad put up his hand. "Sir, see that bit aboot sperm leaving the penis - well I can dae that with my hand" After a short pause I burst out laughing. I have told this story many times and I always say that the class shouted out in unison, "You wee wanker". That did not happen but it does improve the story.

When I look back on the happy five years I spent at Portobello High my memories of staff football always bring a smile to my face. Every summer term all the secondary schools in Edinburgh took part in a staff football league. Portobello had a huge staff and therefore some young fit teachers who could play a bit. In that category were John Britton (more of him later), Phil Sinclair, Charlie Tulloch, Paul Thompson, Robin Ford, Ronnie Jeffries and Bob Paterson - well, maybe not Bob - he was keen but hopeless. In Jim Telfer at centre half we had a frightener nonpareil, who would shout to me if we were not doing well, "Terry, get them fucking going". I was the player manager with "Big Phil" my right hand man. My team talk was usually along the lines of, "Right, you pass to me, Phil, Ronnie or Charlie whenever you can but (pointing) you never pass to him, him or him and especially try not to pass to Bob". In all my years as a player I was sent off only once (got off on appeal) but in these staff matches, for some reason, I behaved really badly. The matches were refereed by a staff member who was normally not up to it and my attempts at on-the-job training were generally not appreciated. On one occasion, by half-time, the poor referee had had enough and resigned. He then put on an opposition strip and spent the second half chasing me round the pitch trying to kick lumps out of me.

In Edinburgh by the early 1970's the senior secondary/junior secondary system had been dismantled and post primary school education was provided by neighbourhood comprehensive schools. Most of the senior secondary schools had tried to imitate the successful private schools in Edinburgh such as George Watson's and George Heriot's. One of the reasons for this was that many of the teachers in the senior secondary schools had themselves been educated in Edinburgh's private sector. Working class association football had no place in the likes of Watson's or Heriot's and it also had no place in Boroughmuir, Broughton, Leith Academy, Trinity Academy or The Royal High School. In fact the only senior secondary that provided school football was the school I attended - Holy Cross Academy. In the all male staffroom at Forrester I was continually in heated arguments with older members of staff who thought that football was a game for hooligans. At Portobello High this kind of snobbery was alive and well until 1972 when a young history teacher, Hamish McLean, persuaded the headteacher to let him start a third year football team as an experiment.

When I arrived at the school in May 1973 Hamish was about to leave for a promoted post in another school and I inherited his team. Rugby was hugely successful in the school mainly due to the efforts of an art teacher, Alistair Cuthbertson, who was a talented coach and whose enthusiasm new no bounds. The principal teacher of physical education, Alex Connor, hated football and he was only one of several male staff who were worried that the young upstart assistant headteacher was going increase the amount of football played in the school. Well, they had a right to be worried. From the moment I entered the building it was my ambition that the school would give boys of all ages the chance to play for their school football team on a Saturday morning. But I had to tread carefully and show that football and rugby could happily co-exist. I should explain that back then nobody, including me, thought that girls would enjoy playing football.

The team I took over from Hamish were now in fourth year and I soon realised that I had some talented players to manage. Six of them signed for professional clubs: Drew Brand (Everton); Ian McLaren (Hearts); Gordon Grandison (Hearts); Jim Bowie (Dunfermline); Brian Ross (Hibs); and Chris Roberston (Rangers). Others that I remember are Billy Turner, Brian Croll,

Jim McGaff, Brian Snodgrass, Ian Gilzean, Brian Lee and Matty Bissett. All of them were great lads and I had an enormous amount of pleasure in coaching them and just being with them. What greatly helped in my goal of increasing the number of teams in the school was that none of them got into trouble at school and that all of them were liked by their teachers. We got to the final of the under-16 Scottish cup and were due to play our neighbours Holyrood High School. A couple of days before the final I put on a light training session at the end of which I gave in to the lads' pleas to "have a wee game". I took the precaution, however, of placing our star player, Chris Roberston, in goal where I thought he could come to no harm. The game was decidedly low key but then Chris caught his studs in some longer than usual grass and collapsed in pain. He was diagnosed with a torn cartilage and, since he averaged at least a couple of goals per game, our chances of winning the cup were dramatically reduced. The final was played at Musselburgh's Olive Bank in front of a large crowd. The match was drawn but we were narrowly beaten in the replay. Although I was massively disappointed I was impressed by the strength and competitive spirit of one of the Holyrood boys and made a mental note of his name - Walter Kidd.

The success of that team helped me persuade the headteacher, Jack Baggaley, to allow me to introduce football into the first year. He agreed and the battle to get football established at Portobello had been won - when I left four years later the school fielded eight teams.

Early one Saturday morning I met my team at the school to drive them in the minibus to Pilton to play Ainslie Park. Only ten turned up and we were a man short. One of the lads said, "Go up to Wee Robbo's hoose, he'll play." John Robertson, the brother of Chris, was 12 and this was a team of 15 years old; however he was an exceptional player. When I rang the bell at 8.30 in the morning his mother came to the door and told me that he was still in bed. My face fell. "Don't worry Mr Christie I'll get him up." Half asleep wee John clambered into the minibus; he scored three and went on to become Hearts all time top scorer. Having John in my school team was a delight that I have always cherished.

Also memorable was a trip to Nice with the Lothian Schools under 18 team when two of Jim McLean's great Dundee United team, Eamonn Bannon and Billy Kirkwood, had to be disciplined (amongst others) for staying out late and returning to the hotel a little tipsy. Reminding them of that has been a great pleasure!

In my fourth year at Portobello one of the two depute heads, Derek McIvor was appointed headteacher at Broxburn Academy and so there was a vacancy for a depute headteacher. I was desperate to get the job, not only because I loved working in the school, but also because inside me there was a burning ambition to eventually become a headteacher and promotion to depute head was an essential step on the ladder. Mr Baggaley and Miss Wishart gently informed me that, at 34, I was a bit on the young side for such a senior position but in spite of this I was placed on the short leet and went for interview in front of the education committee. I knew that I was an outsider for the post and so, at the interview, I did all I could to impress. I was not successful and later met in a pub a parent who had been on the interviewing committee. He told me that I had come across as "brash" which was probably a fair comment. The successful applicant was Jack Perry who had been working in a council education office in England and who, I later found out, was actually younger than me. "I did not get the job because I was too young and then they appoint someone fucking younger than me" was a sentence I uttered frequently at that time.

The day after the interview Mr Baggaley came to see me and nervously informed me that Jack Perry did not know anything about timetabling and that, if I stayed a year and showed him how to construct the timetable, he would do everything in his power to help me get promoted. Never one to act against my best interests I answered "yes" and, guess what, Jack Perry and I became great pals and a year or so later, with the support of Mr Baggaley, I was appointed depute rector at Trinity Academy.

Newtongrange Star

In May 1974 I received a phone call from a teaching colleague, Bobby Hogg, who played in goal for Newtongrange Star, telling me that they had been relegated from the top league and had sacked their coach and that I should apply for the job. I was 31, without a club having been released by Stirling Albion, and keen to take steps towards my goal of becoming a football manager. I contacted the secretary of Newtongrange and was invited along for an interview.

There was, however, a problem; junior teams did not have a manager and recruitment of players and team selection were duties of the committee which at Newtongrange numbered 18. It was the coach's job to train the players and run the team on match days. This was not a system that I was prepared to work under and at my interview I stressed to the committee that I would come only if I had sole responsibility for player recruitment and team selection. Reluctantly the committee agreed to my conditions and I became player-manager of Newtongrange Star.

Right away I was faced with the problem that we had only eight signed players: Bobby Hogg, Alan Liddle, Eddie Carnegie, Tom Cropley, Matty Sproull, Kenny Russell, Colin Wood and flying winger Ian Anderson, who worked in the Hebrides and was seldom available. To add to my problems Matty was recovering from a serious knee injury and most of them were defenders - but they were good players.

I then did one of the best pieces of business I ever did as a manager. The star of my school team Chris Robertson had left school to join Rangers. During the summer he had a cartilage operation and was now fit. I knew Rangers' manager, Jock Wallace, from his time at Berwick Rangers, and I phoned him and begged him to let me have Chris for a season stressing that playing junior football would be great experience for the 16 year old. To my delight and amazement he agreed and, since I was player-manager, Chris and I were now teammates.

Most evenings I was at a youth football match looking for talent and I had become friendly with a Celtic scout, John Butler. They had an 18 year old forward, Alan Duthie, whom they were putting out to junior football and I persuaded John to let me have him. I now had two strikers and things were looking up. I signed Charlie Murphy whom I had played with at Stirling and Alan McLeod who had been in my school team at Forrester.

My last signing was someone who had never really played football. John Britton worked in the Physical Education department at Portobello and played with me in the staff team. He was Scotland's doubles champion at badminton and played rugby for Trinity Academy FP's and was one of the most talented athletes I have ever seen with amazing hand to eye co-ordination. He was as fast as he was fit and he became a Newtongrange Star player. After one Scottish junior cup tie he was rushed to Meadowbank Stadium to play in the final of the Scottish badminton doubles. At the end of the season he emigrated to the USA, played professional soccer there and represented the USA at badminton many times. He now lives in Los Angeles and is soccer coach at El Camino College and is one of my closest friends whom I see at least a couple of times a year.

Managing a football team is a lonely job and the disappointment of defeat can be a heavy weight. I was fortunate that during my time at Newtongrange I had Malcolm Bogie as my assistant. He was hugely encouraging and supportive and, as I was playing, he had to make decisions with regard to substitutions. Looking back I was probably not appreciative enough of all he did for me but I am eternally grateful for the support he gave me.

At Newtongrange I learned a lot about how to handle players. One of the most difficult things you do as a football manager is dropping players from the team. The disappointment of not being selected is difficult to handle and this is particularly true for older players who, as they get close to the end of their career, cherish every match they play. Matty Sproull was in this category. He played his heart out when in the team and was hugely disappointed when not selected. I did not handle him well in that I was inconsistent in my team selection and not always managerial in the way I spoke to him. Also, I was also not nearly firm enough with him. A few months ago I met him for the first time for many years. We apologised to each other for the grief we caused each other, had a hug, and made up. I left him with a tear in my eye but felt so much better for his friendliness and his willingness to put behind him the hurt of yesterday.

My experience with Matty toughened me up. In future I made sure that there was always a gap between me and the players and that they would think twice before questioning my decisions. Some years later I made it a rule that no player could speak to me about team selection on the day of a game. This was one of the wisest things I ever did, because too often as a young manager, you were worrying about your answer to the question "Why was I dropped?" instead of concentrating on how to win the match. Players were allowed to ask the question on training nights but were usually disappointed in my answer. I was always aware that non-selected players might be needed in a couple of weeks and I never said anything to undermine their confidence. Usually I told them that they had been unlucky not to be selected, to be patient and that they would get their chance in the team.

As a teacher I had learned the importance of preparing well for a lesson and I took this with me into football management. I had a written schedule for all my training sessions and every Friday night I would write out my team-talk detailing what was expected of each player. As time went on I also gave each individual his duties at set plays such as corner kicks and free kicks. Nowadays, before matches, the big clubs issue each player with a booklet so that they are clear of what is expected of them at set plays. But in 1974 no manager was doing this and I quickly gained the reputation of treating my players as robots - which bothered me not one bit.

What did bother me was the weekly meetings I had with the 18 man committee. Newtongrange was a mining village built around the famous Lady Victoria pit. When I became manager the pit was just about closed down but nearly all of the committee had been miners and were all strong, straight shooting characters; a spade was most definitely a "a bloody shovel". I would spend much of every Sunday preparing what I was going to say at Monday's meeting. Actually the meetings became quite enjoyable and I was greatly helped by the support I received from the chairman, John Quinn, and the secretary Les Porteous, who later became secretary of Hearts. The experience I gained in handling a committee stood me in good stead in future years in both football and teaching.

My first game as a manager was at Bo'ness; I was playing in midfield and I was amazed at the pace of the game and was struggling to cope. We were behind at half-time but thankfully things slowed down in the second half and we played better and won reasonably comfortably. From then on we did well and ended up getting promoted and winning the East of Scotland Cup defeating Broxburn Athletic in the final. We also had a great run in the Scottish junior cup and were narrowly defeated away from home by Kilbirnie Ladeside in the quarter-finals. Winning the East of Scotland Cup meant that we qualified for the national Dryborough Cup which we won, defeating Petershill at Cumbernauld. This was the first time an east of Scotland team had won the trophy and that Saturday night there was a memorable celebration in Newtongrange.

In the four years I managed Newtongrange I had three exceptional players:

Tom Cropley was my captain and was a real leader. He played at centre-back but was great on the ball and regularly scored with free kicks. He was very proud of his younger brother Alex who played for Hibs, Arsenal and Aston Villa. Tom was troubled with a bad back, which was the only thing that prevented him achieving more in football.

Walter Kidd had caught my eye as a 16 year old when he played right back against my Portobello school team. He signed for Celtic and I persuaded them to let me have him for a season and so he joined Newtongrange aged 18. Looking back Walter was the most aggressive player I ever managed. He was brought up in the Inch housing scheme on the south side of Edinburgh and many years later I was to manage another boy from that area, Walter's pal Eamonn Bannon, who was only slightly less competitive than Walter. After his year with me Celtic released him but he was snapped up by Hearts for whom he played 365 games.

I signed **James "Jaz" Pryde** without ever having seen him play. After a disappointing second season I was in no position to argue when the committee en masse told me that I had to sign Jaz, who had just been released by Cowdenbeath. I organised a pre-season friendly with Willie Pearson's Easthouses Boys Club. We took the kick-off and the ball was passed to Jaz who dribbled past about six opponents before hammering the ball into the net. "Wow", thought I, but there was a downside - Jaz liked a drink. He never missed training but sometimes was happier than was normal! We had a match on a Sunday and he turned up the worse for wear. He was our star player and so I played him, which was a big mistake, and he was soon substituted. Jaz had great skill and a massive love of the game and, if he had applied himself, he would have had a successful career as a full-time footballer.

I had four happy years at Newtongrange and generally had a good relationship with the committee - except for two occasions. The first of these was when they decided to give the players what I thought was a less than generous bonus for a cup-final. I stormed out of a meeting with them muttering under my breath "a shower of miserable bastards". Unfortunately the words were overheard and reported to the committee who summoned me and asked for an apology. I said "sorry" for the use of the love-child word but stood by the adjective "miserable". The second occasion was at the end of my third season when we had been very successful. I was being paid £10 per week and thought I deserved a rise to £12 per week. The committee voted against any increase and again I left the meeting markedly less than gruntled and informed them that I was resigning. When I arrived home the phone rang and

I was told that there had been a change of heart and I was to receive the increase.

A happy memory I have from my time in junior football was being appointed manager of the Scottish junior team in 1978 for a match against Wales in Ryhl. Although we were defeated it was a hugely enjoyable experience and it did give me a chance to manage Rab Aitchison, whom I appointed captain for the game. Rab played for many years for Bonnyrigg Rose and was, in my opinion, one of the best players ever to play junior football (excluding youngsters who were farmed out early in their careers). His control of the ball was superb and he was a fine passer. In 1978 he captained Bonnyrigg to success in the Scottish Junior Cup - a fitting end to his career.

I loved my time at Newtongrange but always there was the hope that I might get a chance to manage in the Scottish Football League. Moving from junior football to management in senior football is difficult particularly for someone like me who had been an ordinary player. But then I got my chance when Willie MacFarlane was appointed manager of Meadowbank Thistle and asked me to be his assistant; and so in August 1978 I started two new jobs - assistant manager at Meadowbank Thistle and depute rector at Trinity Academy.

Trinity Academy

Prior to 1974 Trinity Academy was a fee-paying senior secondary school run by Edinburgh Council. In this respect it was exactly the same as the Royal High School. Bill Brodie was appointed rector in 1969 and he was distraught when, in 1974, the nature of the school was changed so that it became a comprehensive. To make matters worse for Bill it also absorbed the nearby junior secondary school, David Kilpatrick, that was situated amongst the tenements of north Leith and whose pupils were very different from the generally middle class youngsters of Trinity Academy.

Bill Brodie was a mathematician and bright but he had nothing in common with the working class DK pupils and felt that with the merger fate had been unkind to him. After I had been there a few months he said to me, "Terry, I have been watching you and I am going to try doing what you do."
"What is that Mr Brodie?"
"I notice that you talk to them and I am going to start doing that." "Them" referred to the pupils!

He was also a hard taskmaster and was forever disciplining his staff for trivial infractions - frequently I was asked to be a witness when he was doing so. But as I settled in I got on well with him so much so that he invited Margaret and I to his house for dinner on a Saturday night. I arrived home late from the football and rushed Margaret into the car. She pointed out that we could not arrive empty handed and so I stopped to buy a bottle of wine. We arrived at his home in leafy Barnton and I presented his wife with the wrapped bottle of "Blue Nun" that I had purchased in the wee shop close to our home. The night went well until one of the guests introduced the subject of wine. "Well, I would not thank you for a bottle of "Blue Nun", said Bill. Margaret and I kept shtoom. When I arrived at school the following Monday he came running out of his office and apologised profusely telling me that he was just making conversation and that he really loved the cheeky little German white I had given him.

Bill Brodie and I were poles apart but he was open and transparent and I began to like him. A stressful time for me was when the Educational Institute of Scotland called its members out on strike. I had been a member of the EIS since starting teaching and I am a strong believer in the need for trade unions. Bill was politically as far right as it is possible for someone to be; he hated unions and could not understand why any worker would go on strike. From my first day at Trinity I had made it my job to get on with him and I was worried that if I went on strike he would see me as being disloyal and our relationship would be permanently damaged and so I decided not to go on strike. During the day of the strike I looked about the staffroom at morning interval and noticed that all the teachers I admired and liked were not there - they were on strike. That afternoon I plucked up my courage and told Bill that I would not be in the next day because I was going on strike. To my amazement he said, "That's OK Terry. I am really surprised that you are not on strike today." Never again did I fail to take part in an official strike.

On my first day at Trinity I was nervous and was soon to become extremely agitated. My office was small but, as I sat at my desk, I could look out the window to my right and enjoy the view of Victoria Park where I had played football every lunchtime when a pupil at Holy Cross. I suddenly had the feeling that someone was watching me and, right enough, there was a head peeking over a hedge in the park and beckoning to me. Oh, no - it was Peter, my off-his-head, shoplifting brother. I snuck out the front door of the school and crossed the road to the park and joined Peter behind the hedge. "Sorry to bother you, wee man, but I have got something for you". He then produced a beautiful leather briefcase and told me that it was mine for a tenner. Desperate to get rid of him I gave him the money and made my way back to my office trying to be invisible. His parting shot was, "I can get more - see if any of your teachers want one." When I retired 29 years later I still had the briefcase.

Trinity Academy was the most formal of the schools I had worked in and I tried hard to hide my lack of sophistication - speaking grammatically was still a problem for me and my conversation was littered with plentiful "kens" and "dinnaes". When talking about my childhood my mother used to say that "I lacked for nothing" and I would make her angry by replying, "except for underpants, sheets on the bed, toothpaste and toilet paper". I also had the problem that in my other world (football) I swore a lot - if you did not swear you were not taken seriously and were most definitely not "one of the boys". As a depute rector swearing was out and without thinking I became bilingual. On one occasion at Trinity, however, I let myself down. I had the task of arranging cover when a teacher was absent. The member of staff chosen to cover was given a slip of paper called a "yuftie" which came from the phrase "you have to" (cover a class). At Trinity the head of modern studies was Jimmy Reid who had been there a long time, was a good lad, but complained at length when given a "yuftie". One day I handed him a "yuftie" and on cue he started to go on about how hard worked he was and that this was the straw that would break the camel's back. I snapped and before I knew it said, "Just fucking shut up and do your job" and then stormed off. He never again complained.

I am proud of the fact that at Portobello I established school football. At Trinity there was also no school football but this time I did not try to change the status quo, because there was no chance of success. Rugby was firmly established and there was no way Bill Brodie was going to give his permission for Trinity pupils to play football. The school did however have some good players. I remember getting on to a youngster for the fact that he was not diligent enough and not behaving all that well. "What are you going to do when you leave school?" "I want to be a professional footballer, Sir." He was a very slightly built lad and I replied, "Well you will have to build yourself up and you will have to apply yourself to football a lot better than you do to your school work." With his tail between his legs and a tear in his eye Darren Jackson left my office.

After four years at Trinity Academy I was desperately keen to become a headteacher and get the chance to run my own school; in 1982, at age 39, I was appointed headteacher of Ainslie Park High School.

Meadowbank Thistle 1978-83

In 1974 all those interested in Scottish football were surprised when Ferranti Thistle were chosen from many applicants to take the place of Third Lanark in the Scottish Football League. The electronic company Ferranti were one of Edinburgh's largest employers and their works team had been playing in the East of Scotland for many years with limited success. They competed with several Highland League clubs for a place in the SFL and their selection was mainly due to the fact that it was much cheaper for clubs to travel to Edinburgh than to Inverness or other spots north of Aviemore.

Worrying about their reputation Ferranti asked one of their senior managers, John Blacklaw, if he would be chairman of the new club. John was close to retirement and was interested in football and so he agreed to do so. One of the first problems he faced was finding a new name for the club since the rules prohibited the inclusion of a commercial title. Edinburgh City Council had agreed that the new club could use the recently built Commonwealth Stadium at Meadowbank and, after lots of discussion, Ferranti Thistle became Meadowbank Thistle.

As a matter of urgency the new club required a constitution and John Blacklaw quickly created one. He did so in a hurry and years later the lack of clarity in the sketchy constitution was to cause him and me much grief. Basically, all those who worked at Ferranti or had been associated with the club could become "Founder Members" if they paid a small annual subscription. Founder Members could vote at the annual general meeting and elect a board of directors to run the club.

The first manager of Meadowbank Thistle was Ferranti employee John Bain, who had brought a good deal of success to the team just prior to their election to the SFL. He faced a daunting task because they had no money to recruit players and took their place in the SFL with largely the same team as had played in the East of Scotland League.

When Willie MacFarlane became manager in early 1978 he took over from Alex Ness who, like John Bain, was a Ferranti employee. Although just about all the former Ferranti Thistle players had been replaced, the team had struggled with their best finish being fourth bottom of the Second Division. At end of the 1977-78 season they were in second bottom place in the 14 team league - fortunately there was no relegation.

Willie had left Hibs in 1970 and had not been involved in football for eight years. When he offered me the position of assistant manager I went on about my ideas for improving the club when he interrupted me to say, "Terry, there can only be one manager and that's going to be me". I assented to that statement but he had accurately identified the problem in our future working relationship. I knew that working with Willie was going to be difficult but I was ready to pay just about any price for a chance to coach in the SFL.

My worst fears were soon realised when, during the close season, Willie paid a visit to my home with a book in his hand. He had been to MacDonald Road library and had taken out a football coaching book called something like "Place Changing". This was to be our bible and all our coaching was to be based on the ideas detailed in "Place Changing". I was instructed to read the book and make myself familiar with it. The basic concept in the book was that, when you passed the ball to a teammate, you chased the ball and filled the space that would be vacated by that teammate. It was another way of teaching players to pass and move and did make sense but it took the concept to a ridiculously involved level and made no mention of the defensive side of the game. However, I did as told and set up coaching routines as detailed in "the book" as Willie now referred to it. The centre-half in the team was a highly educated lad, David Wight, who was a fierce defender but to whom the "place changing" concept had no relevance and so during these sessions he was instructed to run round the stadium track by himself.

After leaving Hibs Willie had become a bookmaker and he would supervise my coaching sessions holding a bunch of betting slips on which he had made notes from "the book". On many occasions he would interrupt the session to tell me that what I was doing was not in "the book" and he would show me his betting slip note to reinforce the point.

It was a stressful time but I had the support of the third member of our coaching team; Lawrie Glasson and I had been good friends at Edinburgh Norton and the bond between us was quickly re-established. He had played for Ferranti Thistle for many years and had served as a coach under both John Bain and Alex Ness and was very much a fixture at the club. His dad, Peter, was a member of the board and a true gentleman.
The club was run on a shoestring as was highlighted by the travel arrangements for away matches. At Newtongrange we had travelled in a luxury coach from Allan's of Gorebridge; at Meadowbank we travelled in a bus that had threadbare tyres and broke down regularly. What made it worse was that the driver saw himself as a football expert and on the way home would loudly analyse the game and give all within earshot his opinion of how each player had performed. What made it even worse was the fact that supporters travelled on the bus with the players. After a defeat and a few drinks in the boardroom Willie would sit beside the supporters and discuss the game and openly criticise players - a habit that did nothing to build team spirit.

We arrived late from a defeat at Stranraer caused by problems with the bus. On the way home the vehicle gave up the ghost on the M8 and a couple of the players, thoroughly fed-up, got out to thumb a lift into Edinburgh. A car slowed down to pick them up and, like a shot, Willie was out of the bus and in the car with them, leaving directors and players stranded on the motorway. To be fair he did shout out, by way of explanation, that he did not want to be late for his Saturday night-out.

During a game Willie loved to be tactically decisive and was always making positional changes even very early in a match. For example after a few minutes he would say to me, "I can see what they're fucking up to. I'll soon sort that out". He would then suggest some drastic positional change such as the right back going to outside left and I would say, "Willie, you cannae move the right back to outside left!" He would reply, "Can I no, just fucking watch me," and our right back would become a left winger. Again, to be fair, we did have a player, Tom O'Rourke, who was comfortable in both positions.

One thing Willie really enjoyed was subbing the sub. The substitute would be on for five minutes and Willie would say to me, "He's fucking hopeless; get him off." "Willie, you cannae sub the sub." "Can a no, just fucking watch me."

The secretary of the club was a Ferranti employee who would introduce himself as "Bill Mill"; everybody called him "Willie Mills" or "Wee Mills". If Willie had a saving grace I did not notice it. He was ignorant, rude, loud and complained continually. He was at his happiest when the team got beat and he could detail how useless were the players. On the few occasions that we won he was miserable because he had nothing to complain about. Years later, when we were having lots of success, he complained at a board meeting that we were scoring too many goals from set pieces. Willie MacFarlane could not stand him and their relationship was not helped when, towards the end of the season, Wee Mills said to him, "Willie, you have done what I thought was impossible - taken us from second bottom to bottom of the league." After a particularly heavy defeat at Alloa I was sitting with the players on the bus waiting for the directors and Willie to finish their drinks in the boardroom so that we could get home. Eventually Willie sat down beside me and said, "I've had enough of Wee Mills; it will cost me a grand but I am going to get him seen to. Slowly it dawned on me that our manager was talking about taking a contract out on the hon. sec. " Willie, you cannae take a contract out on the secretary." "Can a no, just fucking watch me." Thankfully it was an empty threat!

When I thought things could not get worse they did! Willie had met a relaxation therapist who persuaded him that what our bottom-of-the-league team needed was to relax more before matches. And so an hour before kick off the players were lying out on the floor of one of the lounges at Meadowbank Stadium listening to the therapist who was trying to get them to feel sleepy. Well, guess what - we got hammered by a wide-awake team and that was the end of the relaxation therapist.

In spite of all the problems the team were well prepared for matches. Willie picked the side after discussion with me and I would explain the team set-up and then detail what was expected from each player. But the players were just not good enough. We did have some good players but not enough of them and the lack of professionalism at the club had a detrimental effect on team morale.

Worryingly I was hearing from players that Willie was not happy with my coaching and that I "did not know a player". Knowing Willie well this came as no surprise but I had worked hard to get into SFL football and I was not going to go without a fight. And then came the last game of the season at Brechin.

We stopped for lunch at Perth and after lunch Willie and the directors went into the bar for a drink (Chairman John Blacklaw was not there.) Time was wearing on and I said to Willie, "It is time for us to get going." He replied, "I have had to watch those useless bastards all season and so they can wait for me." The result was that we were late arriving at Brechin and, not surprisingly, were well beaten. After the match there was a fiasco. Since it was the last game of the season the players had to be informed whether or not they were being retained or freed. In a well run club this news is given to the players before the end of the season but that was not Willie's way of doing things and he asked the players to come and see him one by one out on the pitch - similar to what he had done at Motherwell when manager of Stirling Albion. When he told Stevie Hancock that he was being released Stevie produced from his pocket a letter he had received that morning from Willie Mills stating that he had been retained. Willie apologised and we got on the bus and stopped at the nearest pub. The drink was flowing and I overheard Willie telling a couple of players that, "Terry does not have a clue."

The next morning I decided that I had had enough and I phoned John Blacklaw and asked if I could see him. He agreed and I met him at his home. I was thoroughly fed up and had decided that there was no point in airing my grievances to Willie because, after being sacked by Hibs he had lost all ambition to do well, and was just playing at being a football manager.

When I met John Blacklaw I told him that I was thoroughly hacked off with just about everything to do with the club and handed him my resignation along with a list of about 14 things that had to be changed if Meadowbank was to become a proper football club. I also criticised Willie for being non-managerial and for having a lack of commitment.

What were my motives? Was I resigning out of principle or was this a calculated gamble to become the manager. Truth is that I was doing both. Meadowbank Thistle was a shambles and I was prepared to walk away but I also knew that John Blacklaw liked me and that he might see me as the man to sort out the mess. Was I disloyal to Willie? Over many years I have given this question much thought and always the answer is "Yes". By nature I am a loyal person and a team player but on this occasion I was neither. I wanted to be a manager and I had an unshakeable belief that I would be good at it - but I had to get my chance and this was it! Have I been able to live with my act of treachery? Yes, but I do regret the hurt I caused Willie whom I was very fond of and to whom I owed so much.

John Blacklaw refused to accept my resignation and asked me to attend a meeting with the board and Willie to thrash out a way ahead. I refused to withdraw my resignation but agreed to attend the meeting.

Lawrie Glasson was as unhappy as me with the way Willie was managing the club and later that day he telephoned John Blacklaw to say that he too was resigning. John again refused to accept his resignation and invited him to the clear-the-air meeting.

The next evening my door bell rang and there was Willie extremely angry and agitated. He accused me of being disloyal and I let fly at him with words such as "we are a fucking joke club".

At the meeting were Willie, Lawrie and me and board members John Blacklaw, Willie Mills, John Bain and Lawrie's dad, Peter. I kicked things off my stating that I had resigned because of the inept way the club was being run and then went into detail. Although I did not directly criticise Willie, I did by implication because many of the areas I was unhappy with were his responsibility. Lawrie spoke with emotion and stated that the coaching staff were not working as a team and placed the blame for this squarely on Willie's shoulders. John Bain, the club's first manager, accused me of being disloyal and expressed his view that I was after Willie's job. When Willie spoke he accused me of disloyalty but said that we should put things behind us and work together. Lawrie and I then agreed to withdraw our resignations and an uneasy peace broke out.

After the meeting Willie asked Lawrie and I to join him in a nearby pub. When we met he launched into a tirade describing both of us as "disloyal bastards". My Irish parents passed on to me their Irish temper and I was not prepared to by lectured at by Willie. I blasted back that he had not shown any loyalty to me by making critical comments about me to the players. Eventually things settled down and we agreed to work together. For the next 19 months the three of us did work together but we were not a team - Willie spoke to Lawrie and I only when he had to.

At the end of the 1979-80 season we had moved up the league to third bottom and there had been a small improvement. Part of the reason for this was that we had signed Walter Boyd from junior club Bo'ness United which was managed by my friend Malcolm Bogie. Walter was a terrific player and became a fixture in the Meadowbank team for many years. In the following close season we made two other great signings - Adrian Sprott and my former pupil at Forrester, Tom Hendrie. Adrian was 18 and Tom, 24, and he had just qualified as a physical education teacher after being released by Dundee.

As the 1980-81 season progressed it was obvious that Willie was losing interest and, although we had better players, the results were not improving. Part of the reason for this was that the players could not help but notice the strained relationship between Willie and me.

In December we drew at home with Highland League team Buckie Thistle in the Scottish Cup and the day after the match the board met and decided to sack Willie. John Blacklaw phoned me and asked me to be caretaker manager and explained that a decision with regard to a permanent appointment would be made in a few weeks. My ambition to manage in the SFL had been realised! I am not proud of the way I achieved my goal and any defence of my actions is along the lines of "ends justifying the means". Do I have regrets about the way I behaved? Yes. If I had to do it all again would I have acted differently? No.

My first game as manager was the cup replay at Buckie. I brought Tom Hendrie back into the team and he was to be an ever-present for many years. The small band of fans who had travelled to the Moray Firth fishing village made it clear to me that they did not welcome my appointment and this I expected, because Willie, with his outgoing personality, was popular with them. We lost the match 3-2 and it was some weeks before we actually won a game. In spite of this I was made permanent manager.

At that time I was depute rector at Trinity Academy and assistant director of education, Fraser Henderson, made it clear to me that the powers that be were not totally on board with having a headteacher running a professional football club. He was actively involved with Boroughmuir Rugby Club and, as a former PE teacher, was sports minded. His advice to me was to keep my head down and to keep my name out of the newspapers. I took his advice and my assistant manager Lawrie Glasson took on the job of dealing with the papers.

For the rest of that season we continued to struggle and finished second bottom of the Second Division. (Above us were the First Division and the Premier League.) I desperately needed to get in better players but we had no money and paid little in the way of wages. However, for the following season I did sign Peter Godfrey from Linlithgow Rose. Willie had sent me to watch him and my advice was to sign him and to play him at centre half and not in midfield where he was playing for Linlithgow. Someone else told Willie "he cannae play" and so my advice was ignored. At the start of the new season Peter was in the team at centre-half and in Sprott, Hendrie, Boyd and Godfrey I had four players as good as any in the division. The club captain Laurie Dunn was a highly skilled right back, we had a talented young left back in Gordon Fraser and Davie Conroy was a combative midfielder. Upfront John Jobson scored regularly but we still could not put together a run of results. We did get to the fourth round of the Scottish Cup defeating Craig Brown's Clyde on the way but other than that there was little to show that I had made a difference. At the end of the season we were third bottom and I knew that time was running out for me and that if I was to keep my job the team would have to show a marked improvement.

Balancing my full-time job with football management required boundless energy and was never easy but it suddenly became much more difficult when in the summer of 1982 I was appointed headteacher of Ainslie Park High School. Soon after my appointment, the depute director of education, Eric Ferguson, called me into his office. Eric was from Northern Ireland and had helped me greatly in my career; he was bright, highly respected and a straight talker. He told me that, now that I was a headteacher, I would have to cease being a football manager; Ainslie Park would need all of my attention. I told him how much football meant to me and assured him that I was capable of doing the two jobs. He stopped short of instructing me to quit Meadowbank Thistle but made it clear that I should do so earlier rather than later. My ally, Fraser Henderson, was present at the meeting and, as I left, advised me that, if I did well as a headteacher Eric might come to accept the situation. Again he stressed that I must keep out of the back pages and so Lawrie continued to be the club's link with the press. I was therefore fired up to be a success as a headteacher and show my bosses in education that I could do the two jobs. But I also needed to improve the team!

My pal Mickey Lawson was at Berwick Rangers and he told me that their manager, Jim McSherry, did not fancy him and that he might get away for a small fee. Mickey was now 33 but was super fit and we badly needed the enthusiasm and goals he brought with him. John

Blacklaw agreed to pay the fee and I had taken a major step in improving the team.

John Salton was well into his thirties and had a long career with Hibs, Queen of the South, Dunfermline and Berwick Rangers. He was about to call it a day as his ankles were in a bad way and playing was now difficult. I persuaded him to give it another go and promised him that we would provide plentiful bandages to strap the fragile ankles. He agreed to do so and suddenly, in Mickey and John, I had two great professionals in the team, both of whom had a real desire to win and were an example to the other players. Equally important was the signing of a new goalkeeper, Jim McQueen from Tranent Juniors.

I had been playing man for man marking in defence but John could not do all the running about for that style of play and so we adopted the more traditional zonal back four. What an improvement that made! Jim McQueen was a huge success and John Salton and Peter Godfrey were commanding centre backs. We were also well served at full-back with Laurie Dunn at right back and Gordon Fraser or Davie Conroy at left back.

We started season 1982-83 well and went to the top of the league with no defeats in our first ten games. John Salton was having real trouble with his ankles and decided to call it a day. His influence was very positive and he showed me the benefits of having a good experienced player in the team. Fortunately I had heard that Jim Stewart, who had played for Alloa before trying his luck in Australia, was back in Edinburgh and was looking for a club. I met him in the George Hotel on a Friday night, signed him and he played on Saturday. He fitted in seamlessly alongside Peter Godfrey and our winning form continued.

Our snow ball was now rolling down hill and I was determined to keep the momentum going. John Jobson had been our top scorer for a couple of seasons. He was a likeable cocky Fifer and funny and was most definitely the "big man on the campus". That was a position I wanted and so I decided to swap him for Gordon Smith ("Pogo") who was playing for Falkirk. I telephoned John Haggart the Falkirk manager and suggested the swap. He was honest with me and told me that Pogo took a lot of handling but that he was a good player. I was attracted by the fact that with Pogo he and I would be starting afresh and so the deal went ahead. It worked out exactly as I had expected and Pogo was a huge asset in our drive for promotion.

Half way through the season we had slowed down a little and I made another signing. Bobby Ford was a pal of mine and taught PE at Liberton High School. He had been a member of Dundee's League Cup winning team in 1974 but later decided the life of a full-time footballer was not for him and went back to teaching and playing part-time football for Montrose, Raith Rovers and Dunfermline. He has the distinction of scoring the first goal in the Premier League when it was formed in 1975. I persuaded him to try and get released from Dunfermline and he did so and became a regular in the team in the latter part of the season.

The last game of the season was away to top of the league Brechin and we made the trip needing a draw to achieve promotion to the First Division. We went one behind but Mickey scored in the second half and we held out for the point we needed. In all my years in football that was my happiest moment. Although we had finished as runners-up we had achieved promotion and I felt an enormous sense of pride and satisfaction. In two and a half years I had taken a bottom of the league team and made them promotion winners and had proved to myself that I could be a successful manager.

The team that day was:

McQueen

Dunn Godfrey Stewart Conroy

Ford Hendrie Boyd Sprott

Smith Lawson

A large part of our success was the success we had scoring goals from corner kicks. In a match against Arbroath we had lost a goal to an in-swinging near-post corner kick and it struck me how difficult it was to defend against a ball fired in at the near-post. I drilled our players on this and was fortunate in that Mickey Lawson and Tom Hendrie were great kickers of the ball and that Peter Godfrey and Walter Boyd were formidable in the air. Up until I called it a day my teams scored regularly from near-post corners.

I do remember that season making a bit of an arse of myself. Britain is full of "anoraks" whose ambition is to visit all the profesional football grounds in the country. After just about every match the chairman John Blacklaw would introduce me to our latest visitor whom he had invited to the boardroom. This tested my patience - particularly after a defeat. "Terry, I want you to meet Rick". Rick was tall with blond hair down to his shoulders. He was complimentary about the team and obviously knew a bit about football. I started to warm to him. "What is it you do yourself Rick?" "Oh, I am in the music business." "Doing alright?" "Yes, getting by." When I left him a couple of people rushed up to me saying "What was he like?" "He was fine, a nice lad." It dawned on them that I had no idea to whom I had been speaking and they pointed out that I had been chatting to superstar Rick Wakeman of the group "Yes". It turned out that he was staying in Edinburgh because his partner model Nina Carter was being kept in hospital because of complications with her pregnancy. Rick attended a couple of games and he and I got on great.

Ainslie Park High School 1982-87

Ainslie Park opened as a junior secondary school in 1948 and took its pupils from the East Pilton area of Edinburgh on the north side of Edinburgh. It was successful largely due to its charismatic first headteacher Norman Murchison. In 1965 it became a comprehensive school and in 1968 Norman Chalmers succeeded Norman Murchison as headteacher.

When I took over in 1982 I was faced with the problem that the school roll was falling. The school had lost pupils to the newly built Craigroyston High School, which was situated in Muirhouse just to the west of Ainslie Park, but the main reasons for the falling roll were the renovation of Pilton and a change in the catchment area rules.

Many of the council houses in the Pilton estate were lying empty and Edinburgh City Council decided to revamp the whole area. This meant families being decanted (usually to Wester Hailes) and causing a reduction in the school roll. There was also a relaxation of the regulation that forced primary school pupils to attend the secondary school in their catchment area and many parents were choosing the newly built Broughton High School in preference to Ainslie Park. When I started at Ainslie Park it had over 900 pupils - when I left there were less than 500 in attendance. For comprehensive schools to work properly there must be an element of comprehensiveness in the intake. Schools that take their youngsters only from large council estates struggle to be comprehensive since a disproportionate number of the children are from deprived backgrounds. Do I have an answer to that problem? I do but the solution would require wholesale bussing of kids so as to ensure a social mix - for most citizens an unacceptable level of social engineering. It would, however, be my preferred option. What about the rights of parents to have a say in what school their child is educated in? Well, I think this right is superseded by the right of all children to have the best education the state can provide.

Off the soapbox and back to Ainslie Park in 1982. To add to the falling roll situation there was also the fact that heroin addiction was a real problem in the Pilton area and often it was difficult to get parents to come to the school to discuss their children's progress. I remember becoming pally with one wee girl's big sister's boy friend - he was the only adult who would come to school to discuss the child's education. I will never forget that little girl describing how one of her brother's had murdered her other brother. "James came in and said to John, 'You've got my shoes on.' He then pulled out a knife and stabbed him and John said, 'You've killed me James.'" Some years later Irvine Walsh was to graphically describe the drug culture in the area in his novel "Trainspotting".

However, on the bright side, I soon discovered that the staff were terrific and were doing their best for their pupils. My depute, Jim Carnie, was very supportive and I was delighted to discover that on the management team was my friend Kenny McLeod with whom I had been at university.

Discipline was most definitely a problem and maintaining law and order took up much of the staff's time. After a few weeks I decided to do a tour of the school so as to give me a feel for the type of work going on in the classrooms. I was pleasantly surprised by the lack of bad behaviour but I did observe that often the pupils were being kept quiet by "colouring-in". Now, if you are feeling stressed and are about to erupt, try colouring-in and you will feel your stress levels drop - but colouring-in was not education and I quickly put out a memo to staff limiting the practice.

As the school roll fell teachers had to be transferred to other schools and I remember having to transfer 13 teachers at the end of my first year in the job. It was a difficult time for the teachers being transferred because many of them had been at the school for several years and were committed to it. For my part all I could do was administer the procedures fairly, and this I did, but having to make good people unhappy was something I did not enjoy. Some teachers, however, were happy to leave and looked forward to working in a school without a falling roll and one with fewer discipline problems.

Maintaining discipline was a massive issue but all the staff worked together and supported each other. One day I was sitting in my splendid large office interviewing a candidate for a teaching job when a golf ball came flying through the window smashing the glass. The candidate dived for cover and, of course, did not get the job - not brave enough.

Vandalism was also a problem and often at the weekend windows were broken. I came in one Monday to discover that 90 windows had been smashed. The changing rooms for PE were an easy target since they were at the back of the building hidden from view and their windows were broken almost every weekend. At the end of my tether I had the windows bricked up. This solved the breaking window problem but the changing rooms were now like dungeons and I regretted my decision.

Unlike my previous school, Trinity Academy, Ainslie Park had school football and once again I was running a school team. Before the start of the season I asked all the boys trying to get into the team to write down their position on a piece of paper I had given them. I then went through all the positions in a football team from goalkeeper to outside left. When I had finished a wee boy put up his hand and said, "Sir, you have not said my position." "What's your position?" "Substitute" he said and he was right - I had not mentioned it.

Early one Saturday morning I saw an example of the kind of lives our children were living when a boy in my first year football team was bumped by a car just outside the school. He was luckily not badly hurt but shaken and so I took him home. I rang the doorbell and a man came to the door. I explained who I was and he said "I'd better get his mum" and went back inside the house. "Who is that?" I asked the pupil. "Dinnae ken, sir" was the answer.

The first year football team that I ran were hopeless, partly because many of those who played were small and undernourished. However, like all players they looked for someone to blame. After a heavy defeat away to Liberton High School I sensed on the way home that they were unusually quiet and were appearing to be having a meeting in the back of the minibus. Their appointed spokespersons then came to the front of the bus (which I was driving) and informed me that the team felt that they were not getting proper training; all I did was play football with them and go on about passing to your own team. At the boys' clubs they attended they got lots of running and exercises like press-ups and it was their considered opinion that my training methods were the reason for the team's lack of success. I thanked them for their input and told them that I would give serious consideration to their views. I continued to coach them with the ball and press-ups were never again mentioned. The situation was helped by the fact that the following week we defeated our neighbours, Craigroyston, in our only victory of the season.

One game that does stick in my mind was when we were at home to Leith Academy in a match that I refereed. They had a star player - one Max Christie who happened to live in the same residence as myself. Throughout the match he complained loudly shouting stuff like, "Dad, you've got to do something". He was referring to the fact that, under my instructions my lads, were kicking lumps out of him and I was giving no fouls preferring to tell my offspring to "dry your eyes". We got a hard earned draw - a great result for us and well worth the damage done to the father/son relationship.

As always, in the summer term, we played against other schools in the staff football league. One afternoon as I trotted on to the pitch with my colleagues I noticed an elderly couple on the sidelines. I felt myself redden and I grabbed Ken McLeod and said to him, "Kenny, your not going to believe it, but my mother has come to watch me play." There was Wee Bridget, with her "friend" Uncle Bill Borrowman, standing on the sidelines supporting her 42 year old headteacher son! I might have had more embarrassing moments but none readily come to mind.

I was always aware that I was vulnerable to the criticism that I spent too much time running Meadowbank Thistle and not enough time running the school and I knew that I was under close scrutiny from my bosses in the City of Edinburgh's education department. As far as possible I made sure that evening events in the school, such as parents' nights, did not clash with training nights but, when there was such a clash, I attended the parents' night and let Lawrie Glasson and Tom McLaren (who was now part of the coaching staff) look after training. However, on one occasion we had to play a postponed match at home on a Wednesday night with a 7.30 pm kick off which clashed with a parents' night scheduled for 7.00 pm. At parents' nights I welcomed the parents to the school and then they went round the school meeting the teachers of their children. I knew I had to be there to welcome them and so at 6.15 pm I did my team talk at Meadowbank Stadium after which I rushed in my car to Crewe Road North and addressed the parents and then rushed back to the stadium to take charge of the team. We won the match.

In September 1984 Meadowbank reached the semi-final of the Scottish League Cup and were drawn to play Rangers over two legs, with the first match being at Ibrox on a Wednesday night. At that time ITV had a popular Saturday lunchtime programme "Saint and Greavsy" called after the presenters Ian St John and Jimmy Greaves. People from the programme contacted me and asked if they could send a camera crew to follow me at school on the day of the match. By that time I had been a headteacher for two years and it was becoming more accepted by the director of education that I could be both a headteacher and a part-time football manager. Permission was given for the camera crew to follow me and at 11.00 am on Wednesday 26 September 1984 at the start of morning interval I was sitting in a business studies classroom being interviewed by Jim Rosenthal. One of the school secretaries rushed into the room to tell me that there was trouble in the playground and that I had better get down there. I ran down to find mayhem - a youth was stripped to the waist and was chasing pupils with a railway sleeper held above his head. (The abandoned

Edinburgh suburban railway line skirted the school.) As I approached him it was obvious that he was high on something but, plucking up my courage, I managed to persuade him to drop the sleeper and leave the premises; this he did - escorted by the local constabulary. Jim Rosenthal commented to me that it was an exciting build up to the big match - which we lost.

It was not always possible to prevent the world of professional football clashing with my full-time job. Early one Monday morning the secretary rang through to my office to tell me that a Mr McLean from Dundee United was on the telephone; it was Jim McLean their manager. I greeted him with "Good morning Jim." He replied, "You're a cunt." Flashback to the previous Thursday. We were in the middle of a cold snap and our Saturday match at Meadowbank had just been called off. I thought the decision to do so was wrong since the pitch was not all that hard and, moreover, milder weather was forecast for Saturday. We had not had a match for a couple of weeks and I was desperate to get a game for my players. I phoned Dundee United knowing that Jim McLean was always looking for games for his fringe players. He agreed to send a team down to Edinburgh on Saturday. My pal and great guy, coach Gordon Wallace, arrived with the team, had a look at the pitch and informed me that he could not risk the United players on such a hard surface. He had a particular concern in that Paul Sturrock was to play to give him match practice after being injured. "If Paul was to get injured Wee Man I would be in deep shit" was how he put it . Forward to Monday and the phone call. " You were trying to get my fucking players injured. The last time I sent a team down there you kicked us off the fucking park." (Not true - Walter Smith was with the United team and nothing happened.) I apologised, "I am sorry Jim, I made a mess of it, send me the bill and we will pay for the bus." "We will pay for our ain fucking bus but that's the last time we will be coming to play your fucking team."

Throughout my life I kept in close touch with my brother Peter and usually met him at teatime on a Friday for a couple of pints in the Central Bar at the bottom of Leith Walk. I remember sitting there with a group of his friends who were faced with the problem of trying to find a phone number. Thomas Fallon (yes that's right, it was Thomas Fallon the well know bucket-raker) looked at me and announced, "There's your man, fucking headmaster, he'll get us the phone number. The phone book was thrust in my hands and I found the number for them and received copious praise from Thomas. "What did I fucking tell you, fucking headmaster". My chest was swelling with pride.

Peter was now working as a janitor at the newly opened Broughton High School where the headteachers in Lothian Region decided to have their annual dinner. I turned up with Margaret to find that Peter was on duty and to make matters worse was serving behind the temporary bar that had been set up. I should have made an excuse and gone straight home - but I remained, waiting for the inevitable. I was not disappointed: he got drunk and came over to my table and started to refer to my colleagues in a loud voice as "guffies". ("Guffy" was a pejorative term liberally used by Peter.) It was time to beat a retreat and, after speaking to the head janitor, Margaret and I went home in a taxi dropping Peter off in Leith on the way. His career as a janitor lasted for only another few months.

In 1986 the Labour Parry gained control of Lothian Regional Council and, after a few weeks in control, the Education Committee en masse visited the school to get my view as to the future of Ainslie Park. The roll had fallen from over 900 to under 500 many of whom were from deprived homes. The exam results were poor with very few sitting Highers. I told the councillors that they should close the school and that the pupils should go to nearby newly built Broughton High School. Most of the councillors were surprised to hear me say this but I was firm in my view that the children would receive a better education at the truly comprehensive Broughton.

In 1987 I became Headteacher of Musselburgh Grammar School. A new headteacher was appointed to Ainslie Park but the school did not close until 1991.

Meadowbank Thistle 1983-88

These five years were my happiest in football but the most difficult in my personal life. First the football.

We were now a First Division side and were playing in Scotland's second top league. Early in the season I made one of my best ever signings; Graeme Armstrong ("Louis") was at Berwick Rangers after having spent several years at Stirling Albion. He was a left winger with blistering pace and was a great crosser of the ball. I had watched him when he was a youngster playing with Salvesen's Boys Club and, when I became manager of Newtongrange Star, I would have signed him if he had not already joined Haddington Athletic so as to play alongside his brother Ross. At the start of the 83/84 season he was not getting a game for Berwick and their manager, Eric Tait, agreed to transfer him to Meadowbank for a fee of about £2,000. As a winger Louis had a problem - he could not dribble. His way of beating the fullback was to knock the ball past him and beat him for pace. I knew him to be a clever lad and a student of the game and, immediately after I signed him, I told him that, at age 27, he could forget about being only a winger and that he would be played in a variety of positions. Before too long I was playing him in centre midfield and then at left-back and then at centre-back and on the odd occasion at centre forward. Louis played more than 600 games for me and finished his career when he was over 40 having played more than 1000 matches. With his exceptional pace and intelligence he should have played at the highest level and I have often wondered how big clubs did not recognise his talent.

Early in the season we were drawn to play Partick Thistle in the League Cup home and away. We beat them 2-1 at home on the Wednesday and before Saturday's return match their manager Peter Cormack, of Liverpool and Hibs fame, was quoted in the newspaper saying, "There is no way Meadowbank Thistle can beat us twice in the same week". We did and again the margin was 2-1.

As a result of this victory we went into a section with Aberdeen, Dundee and St Johnstone. This meant two matches against the man who was the talk of Scottish football. Alex Ferguson is a year older than me and we started our managerial careers at the same time in 1978, (his first job was at East Stirling and mine at Newtongrange Star) and that is about all I have in common with Britain's best ever football manager. When I took Meadowbank to Pittodrie on a Wednesday night in August 1983 we were about to face the holders of the European Cup Winners Cup who, a few months earlier, had defeated Real Madrid in the final. I knew Alex from coaching courses at Largs and he gave me a warm welcome as we chatted over a cup of tea in his office; he could not have been nicer. The match started and I had drilled my lads to make it difficult as possible for Aberdeen. Alex did not like what he was seeing and started to shout at referee George Smith that we were ruining the match, wasting time and generally were playing in a way that "would get fitba stopped". At half-time it was 0-0 and Alex stormed into the referee's room obviously to give vent to his opinion that we were spoiling the match. I should have joined him there to put my side of the argument but I bottled it being too timid to take on the great man. In the second half the referee's attitude changed towards us - Fergie had done his job well. We were beaten 4-0 but I learned a lesson that day and never again was I shy in promoting the interests of my team.

Later that season we were drawn to play St Mirren at home in the third round of the Scottish Cup. We held them to a no scoring draw and then drew 2-2 in the replay at Love Street. In those days there were no penalty shoot-outs and a second replay was required. John Greig, at that time manager of Rangers, tossed the coin, I guessed correctly and so the third match was at Meadowbank Stadium. The problem was that I did not have a goalkeeper. Jim McQueen had joined the fire brigade and was required to be on a residential course as part of his training. I met with the head of the fire service in Edinburgh but my pleas to him fell on deaf ears. Jim was our only keeper and, under Scottish Football Association rules, I was not allowed to sign another professional keeper. I phoned the SFA many times pleading, without success, that an exception to the rule be made. Eventually I had to admit defeat and at 11.30 pm on the night before the match I was knocking on the door of my pal George McCann asking him to allow me to play the goalkeeper of his amateur team, Links United. Thankfully George agreed and Ricky Clarkson was thrown in at the deep end. He played well but we were narrowly defeated 2-1 in spite of the fact that we went ahead through a Chris Robertson goal. Our centre-half, Peter Godfrey, was outstanding in the three matches against St Mirren and a few months later their manager, Alex Millar, paid Meadowbank something like £40,000 for his transfer.

At the end of the 1983/84 we finished 11th in the 14 team First Division and the goal of staying up had been achieved. During the close season I signed Alan Lawrence from Easthouses Boys' Club. "Nipper" went on to have a long and successful career with Dundee, Hearts and Airdrie. We started the season with a bang defeating Morton, Hibs and then St Johnstone in the League Cup. Beating Hibs at Easter Road was beyond my wildest dreams and we followed this up a with win over St Johnstone at a packed Meadowbank Stadium. We were now in the semi-final of the League Cup and I could not believe that we had been so successful in such a short period of time. In the semi-final we played Rangers home and away and although we were beaten 4-0 in the first match at Ibrox, we did draw 1-1 in the second game that, for safety reasons, was played at Tynecastle rather than Meadowbank Stadium. Only an injury time Ally McCoist goal prevented us winning.

Our efforts in the League Cup took a lot out of our small player pool and we struggled in the league for the rest of the season and finished second bottom and were relegated. Normally when a team is relegated the manager's job is at risk. This was not the case at Meadowbank. After our promotion chairman John

Blacklaw had asked me to join the board and I agreed to do so. John Bain had left to work in England and, as well as John Blacklaw and I, the other two members on the board were Bill Mill and Lawrie Glasson's dad Peter. John Blacklaw was delighted with the progress the club was making and he very much left me to get on with running the team. I was in the lucky position of knowing that a few bad results would not threaten my position at the club.

At the start of the next season I was in Leslies Bar one Tuesday night after training, when my pal Bobby Ford, who was assistant manager of Cowdenbeath, mentioned, that on Wednesday, they were giving a trial to Darren Jackson who had been a pupil of mine at Trinity Academy. He was playing for Cowdenbeath reserves against Dunfermline at East End Park. As a boy Darren had been very slight but had great talent and my ears pricked up. Next evening Tom McLaren and I were sitting in the stand at Dunfermline trying to be inconspicuous. Darren was outstanding. At the time he was playing juvenile football with Melbourne Thistle but had signed a form with junior team Broxburn Athletic who had first call on him and who would have to be compensated if he were to go senior. I had spotted Jim MacKinnon, the Broxburn secretary, in the stand and at half-time told him that I would pay whatever sum he was looking for. Darren became a Meadowbank player and went on to earn 28 caps for Scotland one of which he gifted to me and which is on display in my home.

In the summer of 1984 I attended a course at Largs dealing with how to be a manager. Jock Stein was manager of the national team and he was at the course giving the managers and coaches present the benefit of his vast experience. He took a bit of a shine to me and I spent a good deal of time in his company. Jock was an impressive character; like most of the great Scottish managers he was West of Scotland working class with that "fuck him before he fuck's you attitude" that all of them had. But he was intelligent, wise and all of us on the course benefitted greatly from hearing how he had handled players and difficult management situations. He was a great raconteur and I was enthralled listening to him and hearing his opinion on the current members of the national team. Graeme Souness was his favourite and he did go on a bit about wonderful he was! The upshot of my getting to know Jock was that a few months later he appointed me to be manager of a Scotland team taking part in a tournament in Amsterdam at the end of the 1984-85 season. The tournament was for part-time players and the three other countries taking part were England, Italy and the hosts, Holland.

Before we flew out from Glasgow Jock spoke to the squad and emphasised that they were representing Scotland and that he expected all of them to behave and not let anybody down. He did say however that they would be allowed one night out in Amsterdam. On that night out two players over indulged and, as a result, on my instructions, spent two days locked in their hotel bedrooms with food being slid under the door!

We beat England in the final match to win the tournament and for me the whole experience had been memorable. Two Meadowbank Thistle players were in the squad - Graeme Armstrong and Adrian Sprott. In the game against England I moved defender Graeme Armstrong to centre forward and he ran riot using his remarkable pace to great effect. I had a great bunch of players and got to know many of them well. My captain was Gerry McCabe who played for Clydebank and whose skill I greatly admired. Gerry was one of those players who had a "no touch first touch" as he always tried to let the ball run through him and use the weight of the pass he was receiving to deceive opponents. Gerry Collins added bite to our midfield and, although a great lad, Gerry was one you did not mess with on the field.

A young Falkirk centre-half, Brian Irvine, did well in Holland and soon after the tournament I received a call from Alex Ferguson asking me about him. He was particularly interested if he would be happy to understudy Aberdeen legends Willie Miller and Alex McLeish. I answered in the affirmative and went on to be fulsome in my praise of Brian. A few days later the transfer from Falkirk was completed and Brian spent 12 years at Pittodrie and played 306 matches for the "Dons". An outcome of my having helped "Fergie" was that he agreed to send his great Aberdeen team to Meadowbank for a friendly match prior to the start of the 1985-86 season. I then let myself down. My referee pal Graham Forrest was getting married in Inverness and I went to his wedding rather than attend the friendly with Aberdeen. Nothing wrong with that, but what I did not do was telephone Alex Ferguson and apologise for my absence. Looking back I have no excuse for appearing rude and unappreciative and still cringe when I think of my behaviour. From all accounts Sir Alex was less than impressed with my non-appearance.

At the start of the 1985-86 season I was optimistic that we would bounce straight back into the First Division. Part of the reason for my optimism was that in the pre-season I had signed John McGachie who had played for Hibs and Aberdeen and who was exactly the type of combative centre-forward I needed to take the weight of youngsters Jackson and Lawrence. All three however took time to settle in with 19 year old Darren in particular finding it difficult to cope with the dreadful weather and heavy pitches a Scottish winter brings. Once the worst of the winter was over, however, they blossomed and we finished the season strongly. I started to get calls from Dougie Houston who had been a close friend when both of us played for Dundee and who was now helping Jim McLean at Dundee United on a part-time basis - full-time he was a principal teacher of physical education. Dougie wanted to know how good Darren Jackson was and whether or not he could play at a higher level. I repeatedly assured him that Darren was well capable of playing for a big club. Eventually Dougie became embarrassed at the frequency of his calls and, when I asked him why Jim McLean did not telephone me himself, Dougie said that he thought, for some reason, he was afraid to do so. I assumed that his reluctance was caused by our last conversation in which he roundly abused me. I told Dougie that Jim had nothing to worry about and that he should call me; and he did - many times. He would bombard me with questions about Darren and the one I remember was his asking me whether or not he was as good as his own striker, Paul Sturrock, who at the time was playing for Scotland. I hesitated to say that Darren was as good as Paul whom I greatly admired and I could feel that I had put doubt in Jim's mind.

A few days before our last game of the season (at home to Stenhousemuir) Jim phoned and said that he was coming to the first half of the match. Dundee United were playing in a meaningless game at nearby Easter Road and he explained that, once his own game had started, he would head for Meadowbank Stadium.

Right enough, just after the start of the game, I spotted Jim sitting in the front of the stand. On previous occasions, when I knew that someone from a big club was coming to look at Darren, I did not let him know in case it made him nervous and he under performed. On this occasion I told him that Jim McLean was coming to watch him. Jim was no longer there in the second half of the match but he had seen Darren play a blinder. I was sure that I would be transferring Darren to Dundee United but I heard no more from Jim.

Our first game of the 1986-87 season was away to St Johnstone at Muirton Park. We won 5-1 with Darren scoring three and playing brilliantly. Early on the Sunday morning I received a call from Jim McLean asking me how much I wanted from him. I told him £40,000, which I felt was way below Darren's worth but I was desperate to see him get the chance to further his career. Jim said he would call me back. He did so and offered me £30,000. I refused the offer and told him that I wanted £40,000. "Too much", he said and that was the end of the calls from Jim McLean - but only for a while.

There are two main aspects to being a football manager - signing good players and then getting the best out of them. I never doubted my ability to get the best out of the players I had; but finding good players was the problematic part of the job. The clubs I managed had little money and operating a successful youth policy in competition with the full-time clubs was more than difficult. However in the close season prior to the 1986-87 season I did really well and made three great signings: Davie Roseburgh, Donald Park and Ralph Callachan.

"Rosie" was playing for junior team Bonnyrigg Rose alongside Ross Armstrong the brother of Meadowbank player Louis. The father of the Armstrongs attended the Bonnyrigg games and told Louis that I had to sign Rosie. I knew about him because I had watched him some years before when he was playing for Penicuik Athletic when I thought he was talented but just too slight to make it in senior football. But he was now about 25 years old and playing in midfield whereas previously he had been a left back. I went to watch him at Arniston and signed him a couple of days later. He went on to become Meadowbank's best ever goal scorer.

Donald Park was 33 when I signed him and he had played just under 400 matches for Hearts, Partick Thistle and Brechin City. He was dedicated, combative and skilful and never gave less than his best. I can think of no player who tried harder than "Wee Parkie" and furthermore he was a positive influence on his teammates all of whom admired and respected him. When he was 35 I appointed him coach of our reserve team; after a long career in management he is now Head of Coach Education at the Scottish Football Association.

I was amazed when Ralph Callachan agreed to join Meadowbank. He had played for Hearts, Newcastle and Hibs and at 31 was still relatively young. Ralph had a sharp football brain and a high level of skill and was one of the most talented players I ever managed.

At the start of the 1986-87 season I strongly fancied our chances of winning the Second Division. When Peter Godfrey left I had replaced him with Grant Tierney whom I bought from Cowdenbeath. He was now captain of the team and a strong and powerful centre-half who was terrific in the air. As well as these I still had talented experienced players in Jim McQueen, Mickey Lawson, Tom Hendrie, Graeme Armstrong, Ian Stewart and Walter Boyd. All in all we had a strong team for the

Second Division and it was no surprise to me when we won our first game comfortably away to St Johnstone.

If I had kept these lads together we would have won our league looking back but I was about to make things more difficult. Darren Jackson had just turned 20 and had got stronger and was simply too good for the Scottish Second Division. As well as being assistant to Andy Roxburgh, the manager of our national team, Craig Brown was in charge of the Scotland under-21 side. He telephoned me asking, "Just how good is Jackson". I was effusive in my praise of him and the following Saturday Craig was at Meadowbank Stadium having a look at Darren. He liked what he saw and Darren was selected for the under-21 team - the first Meadowbank player to be involved at that level.

I was happy at having a player as good as Darren in my team but the better he played the more uncomfortable I became; it was just not right that someone with his talent should be playing part-time football in the Scottish Second Division. And then my worries were over. One October afternoon whilst sitting in my office at Ainslie Park High School I got a call from a director of Newcastle United informing me that they wanted to buy Darren. After a short conversation we agreed a fee of £70,000 plus various add-ons if he were successful. I accepted such a modest fee because I did not want to endanger the move. After school I picked Darren up at his mother's house and drove him to Coldstream to the home of the Newcastle director. No agents were involved - I advised Darren on his contract as he knew that I was interested only in doing the best for him.

When we drove back to Edinburgh we went to Darren's dad's bowling club in London Road. I will never forget that occasion. Darren's dad, Addy, was a good friend of mine and it was a privilege to share his happiness. Addy had great faith in Darren's ability and he was overjoyed to see his son get the chance he deserved. When Darren and I walked into the bowling club there was clapping and cheering and all present were delighted for both Darren and Addy.

Shortly after Darren's departure to Newcastle I used some of the transfer fee to buy Victor Kasule from Albion Rovers who at the time was the only black player in the Scottish Football League. It was hugely disappointing to hear him suffer racial abuse at away games but it never seemed to bother Victor who was extrovert, good-natured and hugely likeable. Victor was immensely talented but he found it hard to conform to the strict team pattern I insisted on and, after a year or so in which he played 35 games, I transferred him to Shrewsbury Town and recouped the money I had paid for him,

Winning the league without Darren was going to be difficult but we still had Alan Lawrence who was scoring hat-tricks with some regularity. And then we played Dundee three times in the Scottish Cup and, although we were narrowly defeated in the second replay, "Nipper" had given their left-back, Tosh

McKinlay, a torrid time in all three matches and in January they put in an offer for him which I accepted, feeling again that it was just not right to hold back such a talented youngster.

We now had to win the league without our two best players and that is exactly what we did finishing in first place three points above Raith Rovers. A win against Alloa at Recreation Park on the last day of the season secured the title for us. There were great celebrations in the changing room and, to my surprise, leading the party was my shop-lifting brother, Peter, drunk and with the arse out of his trousers. He managed to get on the team bus and, what should have been a happy occasion for me, was proving to be the opposite as I worried about getting him home to Leith.

When we arrived in Edinburgh I hustled him off the bus and into my car and dropped him off at the bottom of Leith Walk. I then made my way to Jackie McNamara and Ralph Callachan's pub in Montrose Terrace where supporters and players were celebrating our success. After a few minutes enjoying myself my heart sank when I saw Peter in the middle of a group of supporters telling them that he was the manager's brother and that I was just a figurehead and that all the important decisions were made by him. He was now very drunk and the backside was still out of his trousers. I heard him describe himself as "Square-go Peter from Leith", a usual precursor to an argument, and decided that I had had enough excitement for the day and so I went home.

We were now back in the First Division and I was determined that we were going to stay there. In the close season I paid a small fee to Hearts for Neil Irvine and signed Alan Prentice from Newtongrage Star. Both these lads were strong powerful midfielders who worked hard and protected their defence. Their presence in the team ensured that we were going to be difficult to beat. I also signed striker Allan McGonigal from East Stirling.

We had a great season with one match in particular being memorable. Our main challengers for the title were Hamilton Accies whom we played at Douglas Park in December 1987. We were held up by an traffic accident in Edinburgh and arrived at the ground only a few minutes before the scheduled kick-off. There was no time for me to go into my usual detailed instructions to the players and, when the referee rushed onto the pitch, I feared the worst. We won 5-1 with Allan McGonigal scoring a hat-trick.

In the end we finished runners-up to Hamilton and in a normal season we would have been promoted to the Premier League. However, during that season the leagues were reconstructed and, because of the reorganisation, the fairy tale of Meadowbank playing in the Premier League did not come true.

The years 1982-88 were my happiest in football management and I was proud of what had been achieved. I had taken one of he poorest teams in Scotland and nearly got them into the Premier League.

We had no money and what we spent buying players had to be generated by me in the transfer market. What made it so pleasurable was that most of the players were close friends of mine. There was never any discipline problems (except for when Pogo and Colin Campbell had a fight at training). Teams hated playing at Meadowbank and understandably so because, with the large running track, it was a horrible place to play football.

We were also well organised. I drilled and drilled the players in how I wanted them to play. Most close seasons I spent some time at the coaching schools at Largs making sure I kept up to date. My pal Craig Brown would find a bed for me (one year I roomed with Craig and Walter Smith) and I watched the students putting on their sessions in the hope that I would learn something. I saw Tommy Craig showing how full-backs should cover their centre-backs. Normally, when the play was on the other side, the right back would go behind the right centre-back to cover him in case he made a mistake. This was defensively sound but it ruled out the possibility of offside. Tommy showed how the full-back should not go behind the centre-back but should stay level with him so that the right centre-back could control offsides without worrying that his right full-back was playing opponents onside. This is now standard practice but was not in the eighties and we used to drive opponents (and their fans) crazy with the frequency with which we caught them offside.

I spent a lot of time on set plays. We had a throw-in routine that we worked time and time again and I remember an opposition goalkeeper becoming frustrated and shouting to his teammates, "Are they going to do that all fucking afternoon". Corner-kicks were our speciality and we scored numerous goals from them by firing the ball into Watty Boyd at the near post. Once at Hampden against Queens Park we were three goals up after about seven minutes - each goal having been scored from a corner kick. Tom Hendrie and Mickey Lawson were our kickers and often they would score direct from the corner without any other player touching the ball.

There were only four directors of the club; chairman, John Blacklaw; secretary Bill Mill; Lawrie Glasson and me. Bill Mill complained all the time and so I ignored him but John and Lawrie were wonderfully supportive. I was in football manager heaven - but it was not going to last forever.

Divorce

Margaret became my girlfriend when she was 14 and I was 17 and we were married in 1965 when she was 19 and I was 22. In 1984 an outsider looking at our marriage would have thought that everything was fine - we had two wonderful sons, Kevan aged 15 and Max who was 12, and we lived in a nice bungalow in Craigentinny's Christmillar Avenue. Margaret was a beauty consultant in Jenners in Princes Street and I was headteacher at Ainslie Park High School and manager of Meadowbank Thistle who were doing well.

But all was not fine; school and football meant that I seldom spent a night at home and Margaret rightly felt that there was little of the sharing and togetherness that are essential for a successful marriage. And she was right!

Some idea of the life I was living can be given by considering how I spent my time outwith the normal school day. Here is a typical week:

Sunday should have been a day of rest but when I was about 29 I became manager of the Lothian Region schools' under-18 team and then later manager of both the under 18 and under 16 sides. Trials and matches for these teams took up about one in three Sundays. When I was not doing this I was playing football for a local pub team in the morning and then, in the afternoon, watching my sons Kevan and Max playing for their boys' clubs.

Monday evenings were reserved for school meetings. Since there were never football matches on Mondays I made sure, when compiling the school calendar, that most parents' evenings were on Mondays as were all school council and parent teacher association meetings. When I was a young teacher and playing for Stirling Albion I did not have to attend all these meetings but I just could not sit in the house doing nothing and, for a couple of years I taught a night class at Telford College to increase my expertise in teaching chemistry but also to earn extra money.

Tuesdays were training nights and a couple of beers after training talking football with my pals.

Wednesdays should have been a "night in the house" but very often I was at matches spying on future opponents or looking at players I was interested in.

Thursdays were the same as Tuesdays but I went straight home after training and skipped the beers with mates. That meant that I was back in the house about 10.00 pm.

Friday nights were always spent at home but this is when I prepared for the following day's match. I always wrote out my team talks and put down on paper how I was going to motivate the players and what tactical approaches we were going to use. I also wrote down the details of all set pieces specifying the duties of each player. My meticulous approach helped me greatly as a manager but meant that, on one of the few nights I was in the house, I was doing something other than being involved in normal family life.

Saturdays I loved! I was up early and off to take my school team. If they were at home I refereed the match and if it was an away game I drove the minibus and collected the small contributions the youngsters had to make to the fare. After the school match I rushed home, showered and set off to my own game. When that was over it was to the pub to chat with mates and then home and a Saturday night out with Malcolm and Margaret Bogie and often Willie and Joyce MacFarlane.

In the 1977-78 season I managed eight teams: Newtongrange Star; two first year teams at Portobello High School and a sixth year team; Lothian School's under-18 and under-16 sides; the East of Scotland junior team (which won the national trophy); and the Scottish Junior side in their match against Wales. I was giving team talks in my sleep!

Reading this it is easy to understand why Margaret became disenchanted with her semi-detached husband. She wanted a more normal kind of married life. For me there was no question of giving up anything I was doing. I was ambitious and passionate about teaching and football and would not consider reducing my commitments.

In the summer of 1984 we went on holiday to Torquay with Max (Kevan had opted out preferring to stay in

Portobello with Margaret's mum, Molly.) and the tensions present in our marriage came to the surface. On the drive home we decided to get divorced and put an end to our marriage of 19 years. I started sleeping on a couch in the lounge. Lawyers became involved and eventually I bought a flat in Leith and the family home in Christiemiller Avenue was put up for sale.

Going through a divorce is dreadful and so it was for both Margaret and I. We still cared for each other but she looked into the future and saw more years of her husband never being at home and I had no intention of changing the action packed life I was living. Since the boys were clones of their dad it was decided that they should live with me but that they would stay regularly with their mum.

I will never forget the October day I moved out. I borrowed a van from Pete MacAuley, a teacher pal, and, with the help of Lawrie Glasson, moved the few things I was taking into a flat in Fingzies Place at Leith Links. When it was over I was sitting alone in the flat and I collapsed with nervous exhaustion. I was brokenhearted and miserable but knew that there was no future for Margaret and me.

I was now headteacher, football manager and single parent. I needed assistance and my mother, Wee Bridget, answered the call. She was still working as a barmaid but found time to ensure that her son and his boys were properly looked after. Looking back I have to admit that they were given too much leeway - but it does not seem to have done them any harm. The one occasion they did cause me acute embarrassment was when I went on the aforementioned trip to Holland and they had a party in the flat. When I returned a deputation of the local residents knocked on my door and detailed the disruption caused. They went to great pains to point out that it was not the kind of behaviour they expected from the sons of a headteacher!

The winter of 1984/85 was the loneliest time of my life. Kev was 16 and Max 13; they attended the nearby Leith Academy and had all their pals close at hand and seemed to adapt to the change in their lives pretty well. The same cannot be said of their dad. All of my friends were married or had partners and I spent a lot of time on my own. Saturday nights were particularly difficult; after the game I would go for a couple of pints and was then alone, as my friends went home to their wives and Kev and Max were with their mum. My low point was, when in the queue for a disco, a young former pupil of mine asked, "What are you doing here Mr Christie?" I scurried home.

My father and my brother were both heavy drinkers and it would have been easy for me to have started spending time in the "Bottom Shop" which was just around the corner in Restalrig Road and where many of my friends from my time in junior football were regulars. But fortunately, I take after my mother, and I am a social drinker rather than an enthusiast. Fortunately Leith Links was on my doorstep and I spent a lot of time running round it and actually became very fit and got close to under eleven stone - the weight I was when I played.

Occasionally I had female companionship but most of the time I was alone and miserable, and then it changed. Barbara Lyon, Mickey Lawson's first girl friend and a ex-pupil of mine at Forrester High School, was going to work in Greece and, in March 1985, invited me to her going away party. It was being held in a club in Edinburgh on a Tuesday night and so, after training, Mickey and I went along to the party. We spent the evening doing what we usually did - talking about football and then, as the night drew to a close, I suggested to Mickey that we split up two girls who were dancing. He was reluctant but I insisted and plucking up our courage we stepped on to the dimly lit dance floor and asked the girls if they wanted to dance. My partner then started to scream at the top of her voice and I said to her, "Susan, I didn't recognise you with your clothes on". It was Susan Forbes who, eleven years earlier at Portobello High School, had taken her clothes off and threatened to do the "streak" at a school disco. She was now 27 and worked with Barbara in Standard Life. I saw her home and went for a meal with her later in the week and, as they say, the rest is history, although it did take some time for her to get out of the habit of calling me "Mr Christie".

Although she is 15 years younger than me we got on great and we immediately became a couple and started to do everything together. Nineteen months later, in October 1986, we moved into the house in which we still live and we were married in 1988, when eventually my divorce from Margaret was finalised. From the start Sue had a wonderful relationship with Kev and Max and that has continued to this day. Sue and Max work together as financial advisers and Kev, who is a journalist with the Scotsman, is happy to have two mums looking out for him as well as his wife, Margo. An additional bonus for me was that Susan's wonderful parents, Dorothy and Charlie, took me into their family and for the past 30 years I have greatly valued the love and affection they have shown to me.

In March 1987 our daughter was born and she has been a total joy. She was named "Carol" after Susan's sister and we both hoped that she would turn out to be just like her smart cool aunt. She is now a language teacher. The boys adore her and the five of us are as close as a family can be. I am very proud of my three remarkable children; but I find it hard to understand why they are so outspoken and opinionated!

Looking back I have been blessed with the love of two beautiful and wonderful women. For 19 years Margaret looked after and cared for me and Susan spends most of her life worrying about me and attending to my every whim. Time has healed the pain of my divorce with Margaret and we now see each other frequently and get on great. Max and his wife Lisa have four kids, Jack, Ellie, Charlie and Cormac and often Margaret and her partner Martin meet with Susan and I at familygatherings. Very modern!

Meadowbank Thistle 1988-92

Everything was going great at Meadowbank - not only was I manager but I was also a director of the club and had complete autonomy with regard to the playing side, as long as I worked within the budget set by wonderfully supportive chairman John Blacklaw. But I did have some worries. Foremost among these was the way in which John had chosen to ignore the constitution of the club. Meadowbank Thistle was a members' club with the Founder Members supposed to meet each year to elect a board of directors. The Founder Members were almost entirely employees of Ferranti in 1974 when the club was elected to the Scottish Football League. John chose not to hold an annual general meeting and, since things were going well, no Founder Member objected. I had been co-opted to the board even though I was not a Founder Member. I tried to persuade John to have an AGM but he was not interested and did not want anyone rocking the boat.

The person most likely to rock the boat was local business man Bill Hunter who regularly sponsored matches and generally helped the club financially. Bill was desperate to become a director but John Blacklaw resisted his overtures with my support. Our success had been because all at Meadowbank worked as a team. It was obvious to me that Bill Hunter was not a team player but of the "my way or the highway" type of successful small business man and so I would regularly stress to John Blacklaw that he must not allow Bill on the board.

The other problem was that our crowds were pathetically small although we were playing in the second top league in Scotland. The novelty of having a third team in Edinburgh was wearing off and, about 1990, the board starting thinking about relocating to another town.

The four years 1988-92 are when I really earned the reputation for managing dull boring teams mainly because many of my best players were getting older. In 1989-90 we finished tenth in the First Division and the following year were a creditable seventh. But in 1990-91 we just escaped relegation finishing third bottom and we continued to struggle at the start of the 1991-92 season. Given our resources we were doing more than well, surviving in the First Division but more and more I would be asked why we were not again challenging for promotion to the Premier League. Who would be a football manager?!

However I made sure we were hard to beat and in that four year period I did sign good players. At the start of the 88-89 season I bought Stevie Logan from Clyde for a small fee. I remember, during his first game for us, Tom McLaren kept saying to me, "Terry, you have signed a star". Well he maybe was not a star but few players have given me as much enjoyment as Stevie. He was your original "tanner ba" player and had tricks a plenty; he was also strong and quick. I loved having him in my team. When his form waned I transferred him to Falkirk, managed by Jim Jeffries, and then bought him back some months later and made a healthy profit. He did not achieve more in football because he smoked and did not like training - but what a player!

When the team started to struggle our captain and centre-half Grant Tierney became a bit unsettled and I accepted an offer of £70,000 from Jim Leishman, the manager of Dunfermline. I then bought John Inglis from Brechin City for £30,000. John took a while to settle in and I played him more at right-back than at centre-back. After a few months he told me that, if I did not play him at centre-back, he was packing in football; and so I did what any strong minded manager would do - and played him at centre-back. Less than a year after that conversation I sold him to St Johnstone for £100,000 and he subsequently went on to play for Aberdeen and is now a successful football agent.

Stewart Williamson was signed from Cowdenbeath in a swap with Allan McGonigal and he went on to play for Meadowbank for many years. He tells the story of the day he was playing at right-back and I told him that his job was to pass the ball to Stevie Logan and that, if he cut inside when in possession, I would take him off. Sadly it sounds like me!

Donald Park, our reserve team coach, recommended a striker who was playing for Musselburgh Windsor boys club. I had a look at him and immediately signed him. Although he was only 16 and slightly built, Ian Little went straight into the first team. He was small, quick and intelligent and instinctively knew how to time his forward runs. I signed him in 1990 and 23 years later he was still playing for Berwick Rangers whom he managed.

In 1986 Adrian Sprott felt that he could do with a change of club having been six years with Meadowbank. I accepted an offer from John Lambie of Hamilton Accies and in 1988 Adrian scored the goal at Ibrox that knocked Rangers out of the Scottish Cup. A couple of years later I bought him back and I was his manager for much of the remainder of his long career. Adrian was a terrific player and had a remarkable change of pace that allowed him to turn defence into attack. He is a gentleman off the football pitch but on it he was fiery and not against facing up to an opponent. Having Adrian play for me for so long is one of my most pleasurable memories of my time in football management.

I also signed striker Willie Irvine from Airdrie for £30,000; the older he got the better he got and you will hear more about him. Left-back Alan Banks was another talented player I signed and, like Willie, I managed him for several years.

Conventional wisdom states that you should never hire a member of your family. I think that is sound advice but early in 1991 I chose to ignore it. My son Max had played for Scottish schools at Wembley and when he left school, at the age of 16, he became a full-time footballer with Hearts. He had the opportunity to sign for several clubs including Rangers and Hibs but I advised him to sign for Hearts, because my friend Sandy Jardine was their assistant manager and I was confident that Max would be well looked after. When he was 17 he came on loan to Meadowbank, played 13 games, and did well. When manager Alex MacDonald and Sandy left Hearts it became obvious that Max was not in new manager Joe Jordan's plans. I received a call from chief scout, John Calderwood, informing me that I could buy Max for £30,000. I was keen to get him but the problem was that Meadowbank did not have the money. Throughout my time at Meadowbank I was paid little, something like £30 a week, but John Blacklaw did make sure that I had a nice car - a top of the range Audi of which my pupils at Ainslie Park were very proud. In order to get Max the Audi was sold and replaced with a bottom of the range Volkswagen Golf. His first game for his new club was against Kilmarnock; with minutes to go we were desperately defending a one goal lead when the ball was played into our penalty box and Max raised his hand above his head and handled it. They equalised from the resultant penalty kick and a father's love for his son was stretched to its limits! Max played for me for many years and it would be easy to say that he was treated like any other player - but he was not. As far as team selection was concerned I showed no favouritism to him but in every aspect of our relationship we could not get away from the fact that I was his father and he was my son. Max did find it hard to cope with how his easy-going Dr Jekyll dad could become lunatic Mr Hyde on a Saturday afternoon. He would speak back to me more than others and I would pick on him more than I would other players. Surprisingly, over many years, all his teammates totally accepted that the relationship between us was a bit more intense than the normal one between manager and player - they called me "Terry", he called me "Dad". The situation was greatly helped by the fact that Max was a try-hard player and a great lad, with no airs or graces; he is funny (usually at his own expense) and so he was hugely popular with the other players. I remember nearly crashing my car on the M8, when, on Radio Scotland, Derek Ferguson (brother of Barry) was asked what it was like having me as a manager. He was most complimentary but said that, what he remembered best, was the shouting matches at half-time between Max and me - the other players just sat back and enjoyed it. But cuddling your son after a victory – that takes a bit of beating! The last game of football Max played was at Arbroath when he was 31. He came off injured with Mr Hyde yelling at him, "There's fuck-all wrong with you - get back on the park." That he did for fully 20 seconds and collapsed. He had badly damaged his anterior cruciate ligament and never played again. Not my proudest moment!

1991 was not my best year. The team was struggling and I could sense that there was a decrease in John Blacklaw's determination not to allow Bill Hunter onto the board. And then I made things much worse. Lawrie Glasson had taken his dad's place on the board and I had two joint assistant managers in Mickey Lawson and Tom Hendrie, who had returned to playing after I had wrongly forced his retirement. I had been close friends with Mickey for 20 years, since we had been teammates at Stirling Albion. In 1988, when I married Susan, he was my best man. In life it is vital to realise the importance of friendship but I forgot that and made a decision I have always regretted. Mickey is a strong character with strong opinions and he was convinced that our close friend, Murray McDermott, and not Jim McQueen should be our goalkeeper. Murray had actually been in goal when we won the Second Division at Alloa in 1987. I preferred Jim, mainly because he was taller than Murray and better at coming for crosses. Mickey would continually be at me about making Murray first choice and, one Saturday night, after a bad defeat, I had had enough. I phoned Mickey on Sunday morning and told him that he was no longer assistant manager. I had given stupid football too much importance and had allowed it to ruin a long friendship that I valued. Mickey was greatly upset and, for a while, when I saw him, things were strained between us. Time is a great healer and for many years now, I am glad to say, we are back to being the best of pals. By nature Mickey was much better suited to being a manager than an assistant, and he has been a very successful one, having won a massive number of trophies in the East of Scotland League with Whitehill Welfare and Spartans. At every opportunity I would stress to John Blacklaw that he must not allow Bill Hunter on to the board but I could sense that his resolve was weakening. Bill was nothing if not persistent. And then my fears were realised when John told me that he had asked Bill to join the board. When she heard the news my wife Susan commented, "Well that's the end of you Terry." In order to balance the addition of Bill and to strengthen my position I asked John to make the club doctor, Malcolm

Morrison, a board member. I thought this a good tactical move because I saw Malcolm as a wise person and a friend and I was sure that he would support me when the inevitable challenge came from Bill Hunter.

To be fair to Bill he did try to bring us closer together. Shortly after being appointed to the board he asked me to come to lunch with him at posh Prestonfield House. Over lunch he detailed his vision for the future of Meadowbank Thistle. He and I would be a team and that he would increase my wages by a factor of twenty paid out of his own pocket. I was less than enthusiastic and he never again raised the subject.

As the end of the 1991-92 season approached we were defeated at Forfar after playing poorly. On the Sunday morning John Blacklaw phoned me to say that Bill Hunter had asked for a board meeting to be called with the only item on the agenda a vote of no confidence in the manager.
I drove to the meeting certain that Bill Hunter and Bill Mill (who would never pass up the chance to fuck you) would vote against me but I was confident that John Blacklaw, Malcolm Morrison and Lawrie Glasson would be for me; and of course, as a director, I had a vote.

At the start of the meeting Bill Hunter detailed what a poor manager I was and then, to my amazement, he was supported by Malcolm Morrison, who stated that "there was no sign of us again challenging for a place in the Premier League." The vote of no confidence was tied 3–3 with Bill Hunter, Bill Mill and Malcolm Morrison voting against me and John Blacklaw, Lawrie Glasson and myself voting for me. Chairman, John Blacklaw announced that he had a casting vote in the event of a tie and the vote of no confidence had therefore been defeated. I had won the battle but not the war.

The next day John Blacklaw phoned me to tell me that one of our supporters, David Baxter, had read the constitution and had informed Bill Hunter that, under the constitution, John Blacklaw, as chairman, was not allowed a vote; he was only permitted a casting vote in the event of a tie. The vote of no confidence should therefore have been carried by three votes to two. I was not totally surprised by this because I knew the constitution was ambiguous on this matter. I told John that I did not accept David Baxter's interpretation of the constitution and that I would be continuing as manager.

Later that day a distressed John Blacklaw called to say that he had received a lawyer's letter from Bill Hunter (the first of many) and it looked as if I would have to stand down. I refused to do so and told him that I would be at training the following night.

We trained at Meadowbank Stadium and the next night John and Bill Hunter arrived to speak to me. Bill told me that I was no longer the manager; John just did not know what to do. He was well into his eighties and all that was going on was too much for him. Bill and I started trading insults and I remember saying, "Bill, you know fuck all about football". He replied, "You are a cheeky wee bastard and I would love to put one on your jaw." I stuck my jaw out and said, "Go and do it and I will get you charged." To my relief John stepped in between us. I told them that I had been to a lawyer and that the matter had to be settled in court.

With the help of referee and lawyer Jimmy Carlin, the next day an interim interdict was issued by the Court of Session, under which I was to remain as manager until the matter was settled by a special general meeting of the Founder Members. I knew my goose was cooked because the Founder Members had been ignored for years and they were most definitely not going to follow the wishes of John Blacklaw, the man who had ignored them. The writing was on the wall when, at the next home game, the boardroom was full of Founder Members with Bill making sure that their glasses were charged. We scraped a draw and I remember after the match one of the Founder Members, Kenny Bell, taking the opportunity to tell me what a bad team we were.

The special general meeting was not for a few weeks and I still had one job to do before the inevitable happened. It was obvious that Bill Hunter was going to have control of Meadowbank Thistle and, given the bad blood between him and me, I thought it essential that I did not leave with my son Max still a Meadowbank player. I informed John Blacklaw that I wished to transfer Max and he gave his consent. After a busy time on the telephone he was transferred to Dundee for the same amount as I had paid for him - £30,000.

On 24 April 1992 the special general meeting was held and Lawrie Glasson and his brother Stewart called in at my home after the meeting to tell me that I had been voted off the board but was to be allowed to continue as manager. The prospect of having Bill Hunter as my boss horrified me and I immediately phoned John Blacklaw and resigned as manager.

Lawrie also resigned from the board and Tom Hendrie resigned as assistant manager. I was, and always will be, grateful for their support. Tom was to go on and be a successful manager at Berwick Rangers and Alloa before going to St Mirren whom he got promoted to the Premier League. He first played for me when he was a highly talented 12 year old school boy at Forrester High and he was still playing for me when he was well into his thirties. All told he played 335 games for Meadowbank and he would get my vote as Meadowbank's best ever player. I see him every week and it is a wee bit unusual that an ex-pupil is one of my closest friends.

The following Saturday Tom, Lawrie and I went to watch a game at Alloa; Meadowbank defeated Partick Thistle 2-1 at Firhill with Davie Roseburgh scoring both goals. This victory ensured that Meadowbank would in 1992-93 be playing in the First Division for the sixth season in a row. Given that our resources were much less than the other teams in the league, I consider this my best achievement in football management.

At the end of the 1992/93 season Meadowbank were relegated to the Second Division and in 1995 were again relegated to the Third Division. In 1995, now a limited company under the control of Bill Hunter (surprise), they made the sensible move to Livingston. Some time later they were in financial difficulties (surprise) and Bill Hunter handed the club over to Dominic Keane. They went into administration for a while in 2009 (surprise) and are presently struggling to stay in the First Division (now Championship). As I write (2015), they have been fined £10,000 by the football authorities for the non-payment of income tax, are not allowed to sign players and are reportedly £1.75m in debt.

Musselburgh Grammar School 1987-98

I was to take up my new position in early May 1987 but it almost never happened, because, just before I was due to present myself at the school as the new headteacher, I received a phone call from Geoff Brown, the St Johnstone chairman, asking me to be their manager. Geoff had taken over struggling St Johnstone a few months previously and was determined to make them as successful as his own house building company. I was very tempted but knew that my education bosses would not approve of my being manager of as big a club as St Johnstone. They were managing to cope with the fact that I was running the local ex-works team, Meadowbank Thistle, but being headteacher of a large secondary school, and managing a real football club in distant Perth – well that was a much bigger deal, and I knew that there was no chance of the director of education giving his approval. I realised that, if I were to become manager of St Johnstone, I would have had to give up being a headteacher and would have to embark on a full-time career in football management. The attraction of St Johnstone was not strong enough and I called Geoff and turned down his offer – now, if it had been Hibs!

Alex Totten became manager of the Perth club and before too long they were playing in the Premier League. Geoff Brown was outstandingly successful as the chairman of St Johnstone and his son Steven is following the example set by his dad.

Musselburgh Grammar School had about 1200 pupils and around 90 staff. On the morning I arrived there I had a full staff meeting and remember being asked by one of the experienced principal teachers, who was also a union representative, if the staff would be able to trust me. That was a question I had not spotted and I told him that he would "have to wait and see."

I did go on a bit at the meeting about teachers having to accept the pupils as "theirs" and not to think that the solution to the problems they presented could be solved elsewhere. I was trying to kill, at the start, the idea that the problems that challenging youngsters present could be laid at the door of the management in the school and that it was their job to do something about it. The problems the pupils presented had to be dealt with in the school by all the staff working together. I stressed that I saw my job as educating and looking after the pupils and I promised that I would support the teachers in every way I could.
I never forgot the conversation I had with Kenny McLeod when we were young chemistry students at university. Both of us wanted to be teachers and both of us were determined to treat the pupils as friends. I remember my pal at Holy Cross, Andy Johnstone, saying to be, "Terry, you are too normal to be a teacher." Being "normal" did not mean that you were soft on discipline but it did mean that you were approachable and that the pupils saw you as someone who was on their side.

One of the challenges you continually face as a headteacher is to be fair. Too often, as a pupil myself, and as a young teacher I had seen pupils being treated unfairly so that the teacher could be supported; I was determined not to do this. I did not fight every battle on behalf of pupils. Usually when a pupil was given lines or detention and felt hard done by I would talk to them and point out that they had not behaved perfectly and that they must do the punishment. But, looking back, on serious matters, I never allowed pupils to be treated unjustly. This would mean difficult interviews with teachers who would sometimes have to apologise to the pupil. Supporting teachers whilst treating pupils fairly was a tightrope I walked for most of the 37 years I was in teaching.

Telling colleagues that you could not support them is difficult and before such meetings I used to be stressed and, on more than one occasion, was close to hyperventilating. But you learn with experience and as I got older it worried me less.

I am irritated by the fact that the status of teachers has diminished over the years. I find it difficult to understand why teachers are not more valued by society. Here is the advice I gave to young teachers:

- Always be present when the pupils enter your room.
- Make sure they enter in an ordered fashion.
- Have a seating plan.
- Insist that the pupils sit in their allocated seat.

- Have a detailed lesson plan and, at the start, explain the purpose of the lesson to the pupils.
- When addressing the pupils as a class insist on silence and make sure that all of them are looking at you.
- Whenever possible the pupils should be engaged in activities and the amount of time they are sitting listening to you should be kept to a minimum.
- Questioning and answering should be controlled by the teacher. General questions are fine but there should also be questions directed at particular pupils. This encourages pupil participation in the lesson.
- Activities should be interesting and should be ones in which the pupils experience success.
- Insist on a high standard of discipline and rigorously follow the school's discipline policy. Asking for assistance is not a sign of weakness. There are times when even the best teachers require the support of their colleagues.
- Know your pupils' names and always address pupils by their names. "I am not good at names" is not acceptable for a teacher.
- Look for opportunities to praise your pupils and always praise good work.

- The judicious use of humour helps the class relax and enjoy the lesson.
- Tell the pupils things about yourself – this helps them relate to you as a person and greatly helps in having a relaxed and friendly pupil/teacher relationship.
- Never use sarcasm and never score points over your pupils. You are trying to get their respect; sarcasm and point scoring encourage resentment and not respect.
- Finish your lesson in good time so that you can summarise what the class have learned.
- Ensure that the pupils leave the room in an orderly manner.

To do all of the above requires hard work and talent, particularly when you are doing it every minute of your working week. Many of the above points were also relevant to being a football manager and many of them I implemented without being open to the criticism, "He acts like a fucking school teacher."

Two stories illustrate my approach to pupils:

- A thirteen year old girl was always chatting to me during intervals and lunchtimes – we were pals. One day she was marched into my office by her teacher. She had behaved badly and I became the stern faced headteacher and gave her a proper dressing down and administered a punishment. We were no longer pals; when I saw her in the lunch queue she ignored me and kept her head down. After a couple of weeks of this I whispered to her, "I'll make up if you will." Her face lit up – we were friends again.

- I was taking a maths class for an absent teacher. The subject was geometry and I had issued the kids with rulers. One wee boy kept banging his ruler on the desk. I told him to stop –again and again and again. Eventually I had had enough and I gave him a severe dressing down. He was upset and for the first time I saw him without his happy face. Later that day I felt badly about the way I had talked to him and, on the school bus after school, I said to him, "Are we still pals?" He replied, "We've never been pals." After a while we made up and I said to him, "What about you saying that we had never been pals." "Well sir, you were rotten to me and anyway I didn't mean it."

Musselburgh Grammar was a long established school and the residents of Musselburgh were proud of what was know locally as "The Grammar". Musselburgh has nothing like the social deprivation of the Pilton area where my previous school, Ainslie Park, was situated. "The Grammar" has its share of deprived kids but it is a true comprehensive school and its intake mirrors the community of Musselburgh. I started there looking forward to working with the parents and determined to strengthen the position of the school in the community.

Before too long I realised that I had been lucky in that I had inherited some terrific staff. My depute was Alison McKinlay who, at our first meeting, told me she was worried that she would be working for a football manager rather than a headteacher. I told her that she would "just have to wait and see". In the years to come I never tired of reminding her of this and have to admit to enjoying her embarrassment and her profuse apologies. Alison was hard working, bright, dedicated to her job and professional in every thing she did. I soon became to depend on her and she never let me down. After about eight years she left to become headteacher at Dalkeith High School and then married and moved to California. Recently my wife and I had a hugely enjoyable liquid lunch with her in San Francisco beside the Golden Gates Bridge.

Walter Roy had been my coach when I was playing for Stirling Albion and I was delighted to join up again with him at Musselburgh Grammar, where he was an assistant headteacher. After a short time Walter retired and I was faced with the task of finding a replacement. On our staff was a guidance teacher who many years previously had been in my chemistry class at Portobello High School as a student teacher. I had been impressed with her then and, in the short time we had worked together at Musselburgh, I could see that I had been right to value her highly. Sheila McIntosh was one of my best appointments. She was a former pupil of "The Grammar" and, to her, working there was more than just a job. About that time computers started to be introduced into the workplace; I knew nothing about computers and I will be ever grateful to Sheila for her help and patience – the little skill I have now is largely due to her.

I was fortunate in that there were many terrific teachers at Musselburgh – too many to mention and I believe that, in the years I was there, I appointed many others who were equally terrific – immodest, but true.

When Alison left Stewart Mackinnon became the deputy-head. Stewart had been principal teacher of mathematics at the school and had left for a short time to become assistant headteacher at Tynecastle High School. I was delighted to have him return as my depute and he still held that position on the day I retired. Stewart is a man of the highest integrity and seldom have I worked with a teacher so respected by his colleagues. He is also a great lad and in his time was a good footballer having played for Spartans (legend) and Berwick Rangers. Occasionally the chat would veer away from education and on to football – but only occasionally.

At Musselburgh I was not required to run the schools football – that was in the capable hands of Gordon Fruish; but I still took a team until I was well into my fifties when I ran out of energy a bit, although I did referee most Saturday mornings. Eventually, at about age 55, I had to give that up as an old knee injury meant that I could no longer run.

And so life as headteacher of Musselburgh Grammar School was great. The school was inspected and passed with flying colours. All was going well – but trouble was round the corner!

Stenhousemuir 1992 –99

I was hugely disappointed at leaving Meadowbank Thistle – my time there was my happiest in football. I was proud that I had made one of the poorest teams in Scotland an established First Division team and I thought that, with my record, it would not be too long before I was offered another manager's job. I could not have been more wrong and, as the months ticked by, it did cross my mind that maybe clubs did not want a smart arsed wee headmaster as their manager. Or perhaps I was not as good as I thought I was? Well, whenever that thought entered my mind it was quickly dismissed!

I left Meadowbank in April and the summer holidays came and went and still I was "out of the game". I spent the Saturday of the Edinburgh September holiday in Southport with Susan, our daughter Carol and Wee Bridget and Uncle Bill and wished I was back in the dug-out. Eventually I got a call from Gordon McDougall, chairman of Cowdenbeath, asking to meet me. We met in Edinburgh's Sheraton Hotel and, at the end of the meeting Gordon, more or less, confirmed that I was to be the new manager of Cowdenbeath; he had only one or two things to clear with the board. The days passed and I heard nothing from him. I then read in the "Daily Record" that Andy Haddow had been appointed manager. Not best pleased I phoned Gordon and told him that I was under the impression that I was to be their new manager. He blustered something about

Andy's appointment having not yet been confirmed by the board but I knew that I had not got the job.

In October I was approached by Stenhousemuir and, after a short interview, became their manager. Stenhousemuir FC was founded in 1884 and is one of Scotland's oldest clubs. Although always in the lower regions of the leagues they are a highly respected club and I was delighted to become their manager. I soon learned that the board of the club was composed of supporters whose only concern was to see the "Warriors" do well. Most of them are still there 22 years later and I have fond memories of working with Terry Bulloch, Davie Reid, Gordon Cook, Martin McNairney, Donald Smillie and the club doctor, Stephen Brown.

Learning from my experience at Meadowbank I decided to make sure that I worked closely with the board and I met with them every Tuesday night after training and answered any questions they had on team matters. I also used these occasions to produce the begging bowl for money for players.

When I joined Stenhousemuir they were the second worst team in Scotland and my first game as manager was against Queens Park, who at the time, were bottom of the Second Division and were the worst team in Scotland. We scraped a 1-0 victory and my first look at my squad told me that our league position was a true reflection of the quality of the players at my disposal.

But it was not all bad news. Striker Miller Mathieson was a surveyor by profession and a true gentleman by nature. He had played for Hibs for a short time and I had watched him with a view to signing him for Meadowbank. Miller was tall, quick, could score goals but liked to have an occasional rest during a match. Prior to my arrival he had been in and out of the Stenhousemuir team. Sometimes a player and a manager hit it off right away and that was the case with Miller and me. The rests became less frequent and quickly he became one of the best strikers outside the Premier League. In my second match as manager we scored seven goals against East Stirling and Miller got four of them; at the end of the season he was top scorer in the division.

Jimmy Fisher could play in midfield or on the left wing. Wherever he played he tried as hard as any player I have ever seen. He also had ability and could dribble; with regard to his passing he had a habit of taking too much club but overall he was great and I loved having him in my team.

Usually wingers are small and tricky – Ayrshire farmer Tommy Steele was tall and could not dribble. However he was magnificent in the air, could score goals and was second to none at protecting his full-back. He was to be an important player in the team I was trying to build.

And then there was Lloyd Haddow who had real ability and a sweet left foot. However he found it hard to play in the disciplined way that I demanded but he had talent and so I gave him a little leeway. During one close season I was sitting in my office at Musselburgh Grammar School when the secretary told me that there was someone on the phone who said he was from the Carluke branch of the Rangers supporters club. More than a little intrigued I picked up the phone. "Are you that Terry Christie that's manager of Stenhousemuir?" "Yes", I replied. "Do you have a Lloyd Haddow playing for you?" Again I replied in the affirmative. "I fucking thought so!" He then went on to explain that Lloyd had played for the Carluke branch of the Celtic supporters club in the annual match against the Rangers branch in contravention of the rule barring the participation of professionals. "How did the game go?" "We got hammered but he shouldn't have been playing". I said my farewells and returned to matters educational.

We had only four players whom I thought were good enough to be part of a successful lower league team and so I desperately needed more players of the requisite quality. There was little in the way of money and I knew that my abilities as a manager were to be tested to the full.

I was now 49 years old and had been a football manager for 18 years. I was confident that I could do the job and I had a well-defined template within which I operated.

When younger I had found it difficult to accept that to be a successful football manager you had to be an autocrat. I was not confident enough in exercising authority and on a few occasions players had tried to bully me. I took too long to realise that to survive as a football manager you had to be in control of all aspects of the playing side of the game and that you did not spend a lot of time explaining your actions. Autocracy and bullying are closely related and I was aware of this and tried hard to be in control without being a bully.

A bullying autocrat is not going to get the best out of people and I made a point of working hard at building up players' self esteem and, at all times, being encouraging and treating them with kindness and understanding. But do not challenge my authority!

An important part of a manager's job is player evaluation. There is no manager who always gets this right and I was no difference in that respect. Obviously, to survive as a manager, you have to be right more times than you are wrong, but one of the most important things is to quickly recognise when you have got it wrong and to take action. I would try hard to have only two categories of players, "good enough" and "not good enough". Once a player had moved into the latter category I moved him on as quickly as I could. Such an approach leaves you open to the criticism that you are too "black and white". Well, I was too "black and white" as a manager but I preferred that to being "Mr Confused".

On the playing side I made sure that my teams were extremely well organised. I kept a file on each opposition team and before matches I would plan out how to defend against the opponents' strengths and how to take advantages of their weaknesses.

I spent a lot of time on the training ground ensuring that my players fully understood their roles in the overall team plan and before every match I detailed what I was expecting of each individual.

I made sure that a player was never asked to fulfil a role he was not suited to but, if I had an exceptionally talented player (such as Darren Jackson and later Willie Irvine and Derek Ferguson), I would design the system of play to fully utilise their abilities.

Many years later Miller Mathieson described my approach to management as follows:

"For every scenario during a game we were given very specific instructions – you knew exactly what your job was. On Thursday nights we would go through the specific things that related to the team we were playing on the Saturday and work on specific drills to combat the way they played. The pre-match talks would involve 40 minutes of him discussing corners, throw-ins, free-kicks for, free-kicks against. You're doing this, you're doing that, you're in that zone, you're in that zone." (Source: "Tell Him He's Pele.")

In my many years as a manager I worked under severe financial restrictions that greatly influenced the quality of player I was able to sign. With this in mind I made a conscious decision that my teams were going to be hard to beat and, as part of this policy, I tended to sign tall athletic players as opposed to small tricky ones who, against strong full-time players, were not going to get a kick of the ball. This policy meant that, when we played teams from a higher league, they could not brush us aside because of their superior strength and it was one of the main reasons my teams caused so many upsets in cup competitions.

Early in my managerial career I learned the importance of set plays; they gave us an opportunity to score against even much better teams. I decided that we were going to use near-post corners and for over 20 years I drilled my players on the same routine. I did not allow any variety and my teams repeatedly practised the same corner-kick. To be successful we needed great kickers of the ball and tall lads who knew how to attack it. When we had these, we scored time and time again, so much so that opponents would get nervous when we won a corner.

Back to Stenhousemuir; I had to get new players but had no money. Then I got lucky! Graeme Armstrong ("Louis") was left out of the Meadowbank team by Donald Park my successor. Louis was now 36 but was fit, quick and bright; he was released from his contract and I was delighted to sign him and make him my assistant manager. I had inherited the reserve team coach, Gordon Buchanan, and during my time at Ochilview I received tremendous support from both Louis and Gordon. Louis played every game and during matches Gordon sat beside me and was my sounding board. He had a good knowledge of the tactical side of football but, what was equally important, was that by nature he was optimistic, outgoing and friendly; qualities that made him popular with the players and a pleasure to work with.

More luck; my son Max was released from Dundee and signed for Stenhousemuir. Adrian Sprott, now in his early thirties, had retired from football feeling he needed a rest after doing two jobs for 13 years. (Full-time he was an administrator with the police.) I nagged and nagged him and he gave in and signed for me. I could not believe my luck because he was still a terrific player. Our goalkeeper, Charlie Kelly, was talented but small; I like tall keepers and I swapped midfielder Bruce Clouston for goalkeeper Michael Harkness who was playing for Arbroath managed by Scotland's best ever right back, Danny McGrain. I had known Michael since he was a wee boy because his parents, Maureen and Jim, lived next door to me in Christiemiller Avenue. Steve Logan was released from Meadowbank and I signed him. I had spent no money and had signed five players all of whom were guaranteed to improve the team.

My first season we finished in seventh place in the 14 team Second Division – when I started we were in 13th place and so things were improving. Season 1993-94 was an important one for us because at the end of it the current three divisions were to be expanded to four. To keep out of the lowest league we had to finish in the top six.

I needed a centre-half and signed Peter Godfrey had been released from Falkirk. Twelve years previously I had taken Peter to Meadowbank from Linlithgow Rose and subsequently transferred him to St Mirren. He was now nearer 40 than 30 but could still stretch out his telescopic neck, win the ball in the air and defend the penalty box. He played right centre-back but defending in wide areas was no longer his strength and so we played a system where the right full-back did not go forward – this ensured that Peter was not pulled wide.

That season we finished third in the table which ensured that we stayed in the Second Division and meant that, for the first time in the club's history, they would not be playing in the lowest league in Scottish football. The division we were in would be more competitive and I knew I had to strengthen the team.

In all my years as a football manager I never had anybody scouting for players. I had a large network of contacts and, because of my involvement in schools football, I had a fairly comprehensive knowledge of talented youngsters in the Lothians. Also the small clubs I worked for could not afford a scout! Frequently, after a Saturday match, I would go the "Centurion" pub in Corstorphine to chat about football. A referee pal, Brian Horsburgh, went on at length about the talented centre-forward playing for Tranent Juniors. One evening Louis and I headed for Ormiston to watch a player. I did not fancy him and, at half-time, we drove to Dalkeith to get the second-half of the Dalkeith Thistle v Tranent Juniors match so as to have a look at the player recommended by Brian. Gareth Hutchison was outstanding and, after the match, I offered him a contract even though I had seen him play less than 45 minutes. He was a shy lad and took a bit of coaxing but eventually he signed and I was excited at the prospect of having Gareth and Miller Mathieson playing together.

In my mind I always had a file labelled "Players I Would One Day Like To Sign". Because of the competition from full-time clubs, getting hold of talented youngsters was difficult and I seldom had enough money to buy experienced players. But what I could get were good players who had reached an age that nobody else wanted them. Such players had to have kept themselves fit and have a love of football that meant they wanted to keep playing even though there was little in the way of financial rewards. I needed a centre-half to give cover for Peter Godfrey and from the "Players I Would One Day Like To Sign" file out popped the name of George McGeachie. After a long career with Dundee he went to Raith Rovers and had just been released by them. I phone Jimmy Nicol the Raith manager to ask about George; Jimmy confirmed that he was "a great lad" and to my question about his fitness at 35 years old Jimmy replied, in his Belfast accent, "Terry, he's as fit as a butcher's dog". I signed George and he was one of the most conscientious players I managed; always first at training he never gave less than his best and was bright, brave and a "team first" person.

At the start of the 1994-95 season Lloyd Haddow was injured and we were struggling for a left full-back. As a last resort I drafted in Euan Donaldson, an 18 year-old local lad who was playing in the reserves. Euan did really well and at the end of the season St Johnstone's manager, Paul Sturrock, bought him for £70,000.

I had signed seven of our first choice team and the only transfer fee I had paid was a small one to Tranent Juniors for Gareth Hutchison – the rest had cost nothing. Our first choice team was:

Harkess

McNiven   McGeachie   Armstrong   Donaldson

Steele   Sprott   Christie   Fisher

Hutchison   Mathieson

John McNiven, the right back, was a man of many clubs whom I had often seen play. When he became available I knew that he was the type of good professional I liked and we needed – he never let me down.

We started the season well and were soon up near the top of our league - and then came the Scottish Cup. We convincingly beat East Stirling and Arbroath and were drawn against full-time St Johnstone in the third round. With only seconds to go we were down 1-0 and then we won a corner from which Adrian Sprott scored. We had not played as well as I had hoped but I felt confident that we could beat St Johnstone in the replay and said so to the press after the match. Alan Main the St Johnstone keeper took umbrage at this and was reported in the papers as saying that such comments were disrespectful to St Johnstone. In the replay at Ochilview we beat them 4-0 and gave the best performance I have ever seen from a team of part-timers.

In the fourth round we were drawn at home to the mighty Aberdeen. The board wrestled with taking the game to a larger stadium since Ochilview could hold only a few thousand and had a ramshackle old wooden stand; thankfully they decided not to move the match.

Roy Aitken had just taken over from Willie Miller as manager of Aberdeen and his first game as manager was at home to Rangers on the Sunday immediately prior to our cup-tie. Louis and I went to the match and sat in the directors' box at Pittodrie feeling very much like "country cousins". Aberdeen played well and won the match comfortably with their centre forward, Duncan Shearer, in top form. On the journey home Louis and I were not in an optimistic mood.

On the Friday immediately prior to the match I was at home having my tea when my pal Craig Brown came on television to preview the following day's cup-ties. I nearly choked on my fish (old habits die hard) when he announced that he fancied Stenhousemuir to beat Aberdeen. Craig was then manager of our national team and was supposed to know what he was talking about. I was concerned that his comments might fire up the Aberdeen players.

For the big match there was one change to our strongest team – John McNiven was unavailable and young John Clark took his place at right back. Ochilview was bursting at seams when the teams came on to the pitch and the attendance seemed to be well in excess of the number of tickets printed. Billy Dodds missed an early chance for Aberdeen but, as the game progressed, we were doing more than holding our own. In central midfield Adrian and Max were playing out of their skins and preventing Aberdeen dominating possession. At half-time with the score 0-0 I thought we had a chance and made only a few points in a light-hearted and positive manner.

We played really well in the second-half as Aberdeen struggled to match our energy and commitment. Tommy Steele scored two goals and we won fairly comfortably with Aberdeen seldom threatening. Over the years I was involved in many cup upsets and in all of them my team had the lion's share of luck. The Aberdeen match was an exception – on the day we were a better team than Aberdeen and deserved to win.

One of my memories of that day was how well Roy Aitken took the defeat; he made no excuses and was fulsome in his praise of Stenhousemuir. It was the biggest cup upset since Berwick Rangers beat Rangers in 1967 and the press started to make a fuss of us.

I tried hard to keep myself out of the papers aware that the parents of my pupils might not be impressed by a headteacher who was spending too much of his time running a professional football team – but this time my efforts were in vain. A few weeks prior to the Aberdeen match I had been leaving the house to go to a game when I realised that I did not have a coat to wear. The overcoat I usually wore had been soaked at a match a few days previously and was showing no signs of recovery. I went into the hall cupboard and there was a duffle coat belonging to son Max. It was a little big for me but I turned the sleeves up and went off to my game. After the Aberdeen victory the papers were full of pictures of me in my duffle coat and I remember waiting for a lift to go to training and being amazed that people in passing cars were waving to me. I am not superstitious but for the rest of my time in football management I wore the duffle coat – just to be on the safe side.

In the quarter-final we were at home to Hibs and there was massive interest to see if we could continue our giant killing act. At the time Hibs, managed by Alex Miller, were going well and had two highly skilled players in Darren Jackson and Michael O'Neill (current manager of Northern Ireland). We started the game well and after 45 minutes, with the score at 0-0, I felt we had a chance. But during the half-time break George McGeachie told me that he could not continue as he had pulled his hamstring muscle. Without George the reshuffled defence started to make mistakes and Hibs ended up winning 4-0. The great cup run was over!

We were still in a strong position to challenge for promotion to the First Division but our cup efforts seemed to have drained the energy from our small pool of players and we ended up finishing in fourth place.

I now set about strengthening the squad for the following season. I always liked West of Scotland players in my teams because they were so competitive and, at that time, one of the most combative was centre-half Kenny Brannigan who was playing for Stranraer. I managed to sign Kenny and now had cover for George McGeachie because Peter Godfrey had called it a day. Kenny was very much "old school" and he never really got to grips with my emphasis on positional play and zonal marking. He also had the common football habit of referring to the manager as "gaffer" – a term (you will understand) hated by someone as refined as myself! I remember him saying to me, "Gaffer, that zonal marking is doing my heid in; just give me a man to mark and I will kick fuck out of him."

Striker Paul Hunter had been a talented youngster and had been transferred from East Fife to Hull City for a considerable fee; now in his mid-twenties he was playing for Cowdenbeath. Although he was less energetic than he had been as a young player he was highly skilled in holding the ball up and I felt he would work well with Miller Mathieson and Gareth Hutchison whose strength was their pace. I signed him from Cowdenbeath for something like £8,000.

Ian Little who had played for me at Meadowbank as a 16 year old had been released from Livingston after trying his luck at full-time football. I persuaded him to sign for Stenhousemuir. He was a midfielder who scored goals and who had a high work-rate; for the rest of my managerial career he was a vital part of my teams.

Our goalkeeper, Michael Harkess, emigrated to Australia but I was able to persuade Alex McDonald at Hearts to let me have Roddie McKenzie on loan. I succeeded in doing so because of the support from assistant manager, Sandy Jardine, and club secretary Les Porteous whom I had worked with at Newtongrange Star.

I also had a look in my "Players I Would One Day Like to Sign" file. Eamonn Bannon had just lost his job as assistant to Tommy McLean at Hearts. He was now 37 and had less hair than the 18 year old that had been a member of my Lothian school's team on a memorable trip to Nice. It had given great pleasure following his career with Chelsea, Dundee United, Hearts and Scotland. I knew he had kept himself fit and so I thought, "Well, it's worth a phone-call". Without any fuss he agreed to sign and that was the start of a friendship that is alive and well to this day. Like me he is an active member of the "never been wrong club" and so we do have occasional clashes but we never fail to "kiss and make up". I had managed to strengthen an already good team and I looked forward to the 1995-96 season with real optimism.

In 1990 the Scottish Challenge Cup competition had been introduced for teams outside the Premier League.

My teams had never done well in it but that was to change. After a bye in the first round we defeated Montrose and were drawn away to Dundee in the third round. Just about that time I was starting to worry about Miller Mathieson – he was now 30 years old and there were signs that he was finding it difficult to cope with his professional life and the demands I made of him in his role as a part-time professional footballer. That night at Dens, however, there were no signs of any of that. He gained possession of the ball deep in our own half and starting running and kept running. After beating several opponents he rounded their keeper and slotted the ball into the net to score. No player managed by me ever scored a better goal. We won the match 3-1 and were drawn to play Stirling Albion in the semi-final.

Just before I left school for that evening match I received a call from George McGeachie saying that he was unwell and could not play. I now had no centre-back because, three weeks previously, Kenny Brannigan had undergone keyhole surgery to repair a torn cartilage. Whilst I was waiting at the Maybury for Louis to pick me up I went into a phone box (no mobile phones back then) and phoned Kenny to see if there was any chance he was able to play. "No problem gaffer", was the reply. Stirling Albion had a tall and high scoring striker, Steve McCormick, and, remembering a previous conversation with Kenny, I stressed before the kick-off that he was to forget about zonal marking and was to man-mark McCormick. I never uttered the words "and kick fuck out of him" but Kenny must have thought I had because that was pretty close to what he did. He left Stenhousemuir at the end of that season (glad to see the back of me) and then went on to play for several more years before going into football management with Clydebank and Queen of the South; he was a pleasure to manage, someone I admired and his commitment to football was second to none. We beat Stirling Albion 2-1 and, for the first time in its 111 year history, Stenhousemuir were in a national final.

On Sunday 5th November we played Dundee United in the final of the Challenge Cup at McDiarmid Park in Perth. United were no longer managed by Jim McLean who had been succeeded by Billy Kirkwood. They were still a strong side and that season easily won the First Division to return to the Premier League. The team we faced were:

Maxwell

Shannon   Pressley   Dailly   Malpas

McLaren   McKinnon   Johnston   Winter

Coyle   McSwegan.

Five of their players had played international football and so we were second favourites. Before the match I worked hard at relaxing our players and I was confident that we would give a good account of ourselves. Our team that day was:

McKenzie

Bannon   McGeachie   Armstrong

Sprott   Little   Fisher   Haddow

Mathieson   Hunter   Hutchison.

The back-three had an average age of 37 and so we did not lack experience! We played great and had a good deal of luck with our keeper Roddie McKenzie the "man of the match". The game went to a penalty shoot-out and, when Owen Coyle's replacement, Craig Brewster, missed, I started to get excited. Eamonn Bannon, Adrian Sprott, Ian Little, and George McGeachie scored and it was now up to Lloyd Haddow to win the cup for us. He smashed the ball into the net and we started to celebrate. We had a memorable night and I could not believe that, not only had we won a trophy, but also that we had defeated Aberdeen and Dundee United in the same calendar year.

My aim was now to gain promotion to the First Division and, although our form dropped a little, we were still in a challenging position at the start of 1996; and then we got involved in the Scottish Cup. We beat Arbroath and East Stirling and were drawn away to Premier League Falkirk in the third round. On a rainy night at Brockville we defeated them 2-0 thanks to goals from Little and Hutchison. That match got a lot of publicity because after the game a disappointed Falkirk fan tried to drive manager John Lambie off the road.

In the fourth round we were at home to Inverness Caley Thistle who were in their second season in the Scottish

Football League. They were a good side, full of enthusiasm and they beat us 1-0 in a close game. We were out the cup and could now concentrate on the league in the remaining ten weeks of the season. Those ten weeks were among the most disappointing in my time as a manager. I felt that we had the best team in the league and that we should have got promoted to the First Division without too much trouble. If we had had a decent run in we would have but after the defeat by Inverness we collapsed. We had a very small player pool with some old guys for whom it had been a long season and we simply ran out of energy. In particular it seemed as if I had squeezed all the energy from Miller Mathieson I was going to get. For four years he had ran himself into the ground and was now tired. We finished fourth in the league and the season finished on a low note.

I now had to try and revitalise the squad to maintain the momentum established. I had a considerable task on my hands because Eamonn Bannon left to manage Falkirk and keeper Roddie McKenzie returned to Hearts. I managed to persuade the board to spend £30,000 to buy left-back Alan Banks from Berwick Rangers and I gave Clyde Miller Mathieson and money for their centre-back Jim Thomson whom I had long admired. I was confident that Jim would do well but he played poorly and after a few months I sold him to Queen of the South. As he got older he got better and he ended up playing nearly 300 games for the Dumfries team. Looking back he probably found it difficult to come to terms with my over detailed style of management. The board had done well to support me with these transfers but shortly after that I was told that money was to be scarce since they were planning to build a long overdue new stand. Although I had not spent much on transfer fees there had been a sizeable increase in the club's salary bill as I brought in better quality players. The budget for players' salaries was reduced and improving the team was now a difficult task.

Billy Harper who had played in my Lothian school team tipped me off that in his Edina Hibs youth team there was a young midfielder worth watching. I went to see the youngster play at Jack Kane Centre and was not too impressed but the goalkeeper of the Edina team caught my eye. I signed him for Stenhousemuir and he quite quickly established himself in the team. As I write, 18 years later, Neil Alexander is playing every week for Hearts as they try to get back into the Premiership. After a couple of seasons Neil was sold to Livingston to bring in much needed money.

About that time I also signed a young centre-half, Chris Innes, from Blackburn United junior team. He was later transferred to Kilmarnock for £40,000 and, like Neil, enjoyed a long career in football. However I now had a young defence lacking in experience and this started to show.

Early in the 1996-97 season we were defeated at Tynecastle by Hearts in a penalty shoot-out in which we were 2-0 up after they had missed their first penalty.

But that was to prove the highlight in a season that became a struggle. We finished sixth in the league as a result of making too many mistakes at the back and not scoring enough goals – we did miss Miller Mathieson.

The following season was even more of a struggle as I simply did not have the finances to strengthen the team and we continued to defend poorly. In 1998 we opened the new stand and were relegated to the Third Division.

Normally when a team are relegated the manager is sacked. The Stenhousemuir board decided to keep me on and I was determined to bounce back up to the Second Division. Economies continued to be made and I had to let go Davie Roseburgh who had joined me as a player from Meadowbank and whom I had kept on as a coach when his playing days were over. Davie had been a great little player for me and was an excellent coach and I did not enjoy disappointing him in the way I did. It was also a blow when Gareth Hutchison was transferred to Falkirk for something like £25,000 – a move I was less than enthusiastic about but the club needed the cash and I was no longer flavour of the month.

It was obvious that I needed more experience in the team and I signed Crawford Baptie who had been released by Clyde and Albert Craig who had just been let go by Falkirk. Crawford was now 39 but fit and enthusiastic. For several years he had played for Falkirk with their hard to please fans and I recall him telling me, "Normally in football you are only as good as your last game – at Falkirk you are only as good as your last pass!" Of all the players I handled Albert is one of my favourites. Not because of his winning ways – he was a little bit on the dour side and, if you got a smile out of him, – well you had achieved something that day. But he was a terrific player and the type you dream about having in that he did not need a manager because he was totally self-motivating. In the dressing room before away matches he would sit and appear to pay little attention when I was going through in detail how we were going to approach the game. As the players lined up to go out a few minutes before kick-off he came to life and always said, "Let's fuck them and get doon the road." I loved that!

We started the season reasonably well but needed someone up front to support a local youngster, Ross Hamilton, who was doing well. A former pupil of mine Kenny Miller had signed for Hibs and was finding it hard to break into the first team. He was only 18 but I had seen a lot of him as a player and was confident that he would do well for us. I asked the Hibs manager, Alex McLeish, if I could have Kenny on loan and, to my delight he agreed. His first game was away to Albion Rovers and he scored two goals – we now had two quick young strikers and I was more optimistic about the future. At the end of that season Kenny returned to Hibs and went immediately into the first team and started to score. In the year 2000 he went to Rangers for a fee of £1million and in a long career played for Scotland 69 times.

In the first round of the Scottish Cup we played Alloa managed by my pal Tom Hendrie. That season they were a division above us having won the Third Division the previous season. We narrowly beat them in a replay and in the second round were drawn against Whitehill Welfare managed by another of my close friends, Mickey Lawson. Hibs had not allowed us to play Kenny Miller in the Cup because they did not wish him to be cup-tied. We were lucky to draw 1-1 with Whitehill at Rosewell and, before the replay, we learned that the winners were to face Rangers at Ibrox. The financial rewards would be considerable and, with that in mind, I went to see Rod Petrie, Chief Executive of Hibs, and tried to persuade him to give permission for Kenny Miller to play in the replay. Rod agreed but on condition that, if we beat Whitehill and got through, a payment of £20,000 had to be made to Hibs by Stenhousemuir. Not surprisingly the "Warriors" board were not too keen on the idea. After several phone calls Rod and I agreed on a payment of something like £12,000 and Kenny was allowed to play. On a frozen pitch at Ochilview (after Whitehill missed a first-half penalty) we won 2-0 with Kenny scoring both goals.

In the days before the match at Ibrox, Tom Hendrie left Alloa to become manager of St Mirren. He let me know that Alloa would be interested in having me as their manager and I knew that the Stenhousemuir board would not stand in my way as there was a feeling that I had done my bit for them and a fresh face was needed. I agreed to meet the Alloa board on the Sunday following the Rangers game.

Rangers had recently appointed Dick Advocaat to replace Walter Smith as manager and had a strong side. Early in the game Adrian Sprott hit their crossbar with a shot but after that we were mainly on the back foot. We played with enthusiasm and spirit but were beaten 2-0 and my time at Stenhousemuir was over. There had been close to 40,000 at the match and the club bank balance was greatly improved even after Hibs were squared for allowing Kenny Miller to play in the competition.

I had been manager of Stenhousemuir for over six years and had loved my time there. I left disappointed that I had never managed to take the team into the First Division as I had done with Meadowbank but beating both Aberdeen and then Dundee United in 1995 was something special. When I left Louis became manager and, to his great credit, at the end of the season the club returned to the Second Division – the first time in their history that they had been promoted. I could not have been more pleased!

Musselburgh Grammar School 1998-2003

In August 1998 I returned to school after the summer holidays in a good frame of mind – football management was a struggle but at least things were good at school. After a few weeks youths from the Wimpey housing scheme started to fight with their counterparts from the Pinkie scheme. They were causing no end of trouble in the community and then it came into the school.

Most of the pupils involved, but by no means all of them, were in the fourth year, their last year at school. Also involved were a sizeable number of youths no longer at school and boys of school age who were Catholics and attended St David's in Dalkeith.

As the term progressed the school became the venue for gang fights. We had fights in the playground and in the school corridors; at lunchtime and at the end off the school day, groups of youths who had left school would be waiting outside the building ready to start more fights.

No one knew what had started the gang warfare but it was a terrible situation. I liaised closely with the police who were frequently called in to stem the trouble. I also excluded large numbers of boys but they would return to school after the exclusion period was over; permanent exclusion was not an option because East Lothian council had no arrangements for coping with large numbers of permanently excluded youngsters.

During intervals and lunchtimes my staff patrolled the corridors and worked hard at keeping the warring factions apart. However, even during period changeovers fights would break out in the corridors. I remember at the end of a school day putting myself between two former pupils, one who had a motor car starting handle in his hand and the other who was wielding the chain from a motor bike. I escaped unhurt but it was frightening and was dreadful.

I had meetings with the parents involved asking them to ensure that their sons did not get involved – this made little difference.

Throughout this time my staff and I did all we could to ensure that the education of the pupils not involved was not affected. We were mostly successful in this but could not prevent our youngsters witnessing many violent fights involving lots of boys.

From experience I knew that these feuds eventually ran out of steam and that the boys involved would find something else to do with their energies. My strategy was to deal with it using the police and parents and wait for the calm to come. There was no easy answer and the police were stretched dealing with the continuous fights at night in the Pinkie and Wimpey estates – fights that would continue next day at school.

The Christmas holidays came and I prayed that, when the pupils returned in January, things would have calmed down. They did not!

At 9.00 am on Monday 18 January 1998 my secretary phoned to say that three of Her Majesty's Inspectorate had arrived in the school to carry out a care and welfare inspection. This was a new type of inspection where no notice was given to the school and which targeted schools where there were concerns about the care and welfare of the pupils. I knew we were in trouble.

From the start the inspectors made it clear that the dreadful situation they found had to be someone's fault and I knew that that "someone" would be me. I was aware that there was little chance of them reporting on a school in which there was warring in the corridors and playgrounds and saying that nobody was to blame.

To write about the abilities of the three inspectors is difficult without leaving myself open to the Mandy Rice-Davies misquote, "Well he would say that, wouldn't he". In judging the merits of a teacher I often used the yardstick, "Could they control the queue for school lunches?". All three would have failed that test. One of them was an elderly lady who came to see me on her first day after sitting in on a modern language lesson. In the class was a girl whose behaviour was on the far side of "challenging". Not surprisingly, with a stranger sitting in the classroom, the girl behaved badly. In her report back to me she blamed the teacher (who was great) for the girl's unacceptable behaviour. She was not interested hearing about the child's background – the teacher was to blame and that was it.

On another occasion I was being interviewed in my office when in stormed the mother of one of the boys excluded for his involvement in the fighting. She started to shout abuse at me and I pacified her as best I could and tried to calm her down. The whole thing was unpleasant but I could not help but notice that the hand in which the inspector was holding his pen had started to shake.

During their four day visit the inspectors witnessed a fight in the corridors and it became obvious to me that the on going strife would make it hard for them to say anything good about the school. They issued questionnaires to pupils and not surprisingly, given the continuing violence, the answers were much more negative than they normally would have been.

On 8th June the inspectors report was published and it painted a bleak picture of Musselburgh Grammar School and referred to my leadership as having "more weaknesses than strengths". When releasing the report someone in the Scottish Office referred to it as "the worst report ever received by a Scottish school". These words were not part of the report but they were the ones highlighted by the press who also made a great deal of the fact that I was manager of Alloa Athletic.

During that day I was contacted by the "Scotsman" who offered me the chance to write a piece for them. I contacted the Director of Education of East Lothian, Alan Blackie, who gave his permission and that afternoon, with the help of my deputy, Stewart

MacKinnon, I wrote the following article which was published the next day:

"THE INSPECTORS ARRIVED AND WERE CONFUSED BY WHAT THEY FOUND

On Monday 18 January I had just returned to my office at 9.00 am after my weekly meeting with our principal teachers to be told that three of Her Majesty's Inspectorate had just arrived at reception. We had got lucky and were about to be the third school in Scotland to have an unannounced care and welfare inspection.

For the school it could not have come at a worse time.

Musselburgh Grammar School reflects very accurately the town of Musselburgh. The vast majority of our pupils are hard-working, polite and thoroughly likeable. The behaviour of a small minority does present a challenge to our staff who, as the report states, work hard "to ensure that incidents relating to behaviour and discipline had as little as possible effect on the everyday work of staff and pupils.

Like most comprehensive schools, our pupils cover a wide range of abilities and behaviour. Unlike most schools, however, for some considerable time prior to the inspectors' visit, we had sporadic trouble with rival gangs of youths in the community using the school as a venue to settle their feuds. Some of the boys involved were pupils of the Grammar but many were over 16 and had long since left the school.

In the days immediately prior to the inspection there had been fairly serious trouble involving these gangs in the precincts of the school and this trouble influenced the answers our pupils gave in the questionnaire issued by the inspectors.

Contrary to the inspectors I feel we handled a difficult situation exceptionally well. Our priority was to protect the vast majority of pupils who are hard working and well behaved. This we have done and their education has gone on uninterrupted. The inspectors concentrated on the negative and commented on little that was positive and there was much that was positive to report.

With regard to examinations, our value added figures for converting Standard Grades into Higher passes is above the Scottish average and departments such as mathematics, craft and design and technology and art are significantly above average.

We have healthy pass rates in most Higher subjects and, each year, many pupils are presented for the Certificate of Sixth Year Studies. We offer a wide range of extra-curricular activities and two pupils from this session's sixth year, Vikki Laing and Lee Harper, are the current girls and boys champion golfers in Scotland. In recent months we have organised three trips abroad and, all in all, are in most ways a normal school.

Yesterday, many pupils felt confused, then became angry that their school had been attacked with such vitriol. Quite frankly, they just could not recognise the school described in this newspaper as being the same one they attended.

I am perhaps naïve, but what I personally have found hard to cope with has been the attack on the school by an undisclosed Scottish Office source. This source made comments about the school which were not in the report and which were never given to me verbally.

I expect Government officials to act in an open manner and not to make derogatory comments to a newspaper without having the courage to put their names to these comments. It is difficult to attribute a motive other than malice to the very damaging remark that the report was the "worst ever received".

Over the past 24 hours I have received very encouraging support from East Lothian Council, the school board, the parent teacher association and many parents. We have a united staff and many terrific pupils and I am extremely hopeful that, next May, when the inspectors revisit the school, they will produce a much more fair-minded and positive report."

I got home that day at six o'clock just to catch the start of the BBC national news which led with the story of "the worst school in Scotland" and making much of the fact that I was a football manager.

The next day the school was under siege from press photographers and the negative publicity continued. However, the feuding stopped and remained stopped. It was as if someone had switched off the "let's be crazy button".

Generally the people of Musselburgh got behind the school. Many of them were former pupils and many had children who had gone to the school and received a first class education. They knew that the school was not perfect but also realised that the picture of the school painted by the inspectors' report was unfair and that they had seen the school at the worst time in its history. There was considerable anger at the description "the worst school in Scotland".

I received a large amount of letters of support and the backing I received helped me greatly in getting through a horrible time. Musselburgh is the "Honest Toun" and a couple of months after the publication of the report I was guest speaker at the annual dinner of the "Honest Toun Association". After my speech I was given a long standing ovation and the support I received that night will stay with me forever.

The report contained a large number of recommendations for improving the school. Just about all of them were of a trivial nature and required the school to have a large increase in written policies. However, I set about implementing all of their recommendations motivated by the desire to ensure that, when they returned in a year's time for the follow-up inspection, they would have little to complain about. I prepared a comprehensive document detailing the changes made. After their return inspection the inspectors in June 2000 gave the school a clean bill of health stating that "very good progress" had been made. I was now back to being a "good guy" and was praised in the press for turning the school around. In reality little had changed – it had always been a good school. At the end of that troubled year the school achieved its best ever results in the national examinations.

I have often reflected on that terrible time and searched my mind for things that I could have done better. I have never come up with any answers but it was one of the most testing periods in my life and I do tend to block it out. During that time I received wonderful support from the staff of the school and will always be indebted to them. My management team "had my back" and I will always be grateful to Stewart MacKinnon, Sheila McIntosh, George Robertson, Gordon Fruish, Ann Graham and Yvonne Mackie. I will also always be thankful for the support I received from the Director of Education, Alan Blackie.

There was one incident that challenged my belief that kids always deserve a second chance. One morning interval a gang of youths (many of whom were not pupils) attacked boys in the playground at the back of the school. Stewart and I were alerted and ran to the scene of the trouble. As Stewart went to assist a youngster lying on the ground a boy ran up and kicked the pupil in the head with considerable force. The boy became unconscious and I dialled 999 for an ambulance. Luckily he fully recovered. The assailant was a boy who, at the time, was excluded from school because of his involvement in the trouble. He had returned to school purely for the purpose of beating someone up.

I felt that the boy who had done the kicking had behaved in a seriously unacceptable manner, and, as well as having him charged with assault, I decided that he had used up his chances and that he should be permanently excluded from the Grammar School. His mother, a single parent, appealed against my decision and her appeal was heard by a tribunal consisting of a parent, a retired headteacher, and a member of the East Lothian council. I argued strongly that, given the problems I was having at the school, and the serious nature of the assault, my authority needed to be supported and that the boy should be moved to another school. A friend of his mother eloquently put the case that he was a good boy who had been led astray. The tribunal decided that the boy should return to the Grammar and I left the meeting with steam coming out my ears. And yes the inevitable happened – he never again put a foot wrong, became a pal of mine and left school with good qualifications. It was an outcome I had not anticipated but I was glad to be wrong.

On a lighter note I remember interviewing a father about his son's part in the feud. The discussion did not go well and, since he was a giant, I started to get a bit nervous. However, to my relief, he eventually got up to go – but he needed to get the last word in and, holding the door open, he shouted at me, "You're maybe a good fitba manager but you're a shite headmaster". He then slammed the door.

I was back to the still demanding job of running a normal school and, as my 60th birthday approached, thoughts of retirement started to enter my head. The strain of doing two jobs for so long was starting to tell and leaving school at 5.30 pm and driving to Alloa for training was becoming a difficult task. I have had good health all my life but suffer from eczema and spend a lot of time scratching. The itch is at its worst at night-time and back then I was doing more scratching than sleeping and my body was telling me that I had to slow down. I started to look forward to having some time with nothing to do.

In June 2003 aged 60 I retired as headteacher of Musselburgh Grammar School. The Scottish Schools' Football Association presented me with a long service award and this is something I am especially proud of. The community of Musselburgh made a fuss of me and there were several functions to mark my retirement. At all of these I was close to tears brought about by the kindness shown to me. I had loved my 16 years at the Grammar and will never forget, on my last day, the long queue of girls in the corridor outside my office awaiting their chance to come in and kiss me goodbye. When I walked across the playground to my car for the last time it was with a heavy heart but I knew that my time was up and that I was doing the right thing.

Alloa Athletic 1999 – 2003

The story of my time at Alloa is similar to what occurred at Newtongrange, Meadowbank and Stenhousemuir and remembering "Rocky IV" I will attempt to be less long winded.

As a Stenhousemuir, I found myself working for a board of directors who were all supporters at heart and passionate about their club. The following all became friends of mine and all of them are still involved in running the club they love: Pat Lawlor, Bobby Hopkins, Ewen Cameron, George Ormiston, and David Murray.

When I joined Alloa in January 1999 I was having a terrible time at school but, funnily enough, the problems in managing a football club took my mind off the chaos at school and helped keep me sane. By that time I had been a manager for nearly 25 years and I was confident in my ability to do the job. As always the problem was recruiting talented players on a limited budget.

The team I inherited from Tom Hendrie was much better than the one I took over at Stenhousemuir. The previous season they had won the Third Division but were finding it harder in the Second Division. But I did have one super player!

Eight years previously I had signed striker Willie Irvine for Meadowbank from Airdrie. He did well for me but now, at 35, he was close to being the best player in part-time Scottish football. He had left Meadowbank to join

Tom Hendrie at Berwick Rangers and then had moved with Tom to Alloa. Tom had changed his role – he was no longer an out an out striker but played in a deeper position off the centre-forward where he could make best use of his sharp football brain. The team was shaped around Willie and soon I understood why Tom had been wise to do so. His anticipation made up for his lack of pace and opposing defenders found it difficult to mark him. I agree that "one man does not make a team" but, if that one man is a terrific player, he can make a helluva difference – and Willie Irvine was that man!

Besides Willie, I inherited two other players who gave me cause to be optimistic. Craig Valentine was club captain and led by example. He was short for a central defender but he was quick, bright and as brave a player as I ever saw. Martin Cameron was also a "reason to be cheerful"; he was a raw youngster but was fast, tall and strong and could score goals. His nickname was "Butch" because he worked in Tom Hendrie's cousin's butcher shop.

At the end of my first season we finished fifth in the ten-team league and I set about trying to make us better.

Max and Ian Little were out of contract at Stenhousemuir and so I recruited both of them. I then went back into my file "Players I Would One Day Like to Sign" and talked Gary Clark into joining up. Gary was a midfielder who had played for many clubs; he was a great professional and I knew that he would give us that wee bit of West of Scotland grit that we needed – and he scored the occasional goal.

I also had a new assistant manager. Brian Fairlie had been interviewed for the manager's job and had impressed the board who told me that they would like him to be my assistant. I did not know Brian but he had been coaching successfully in junior football for a number of years and I immediately agreed to the board's proposal and phoned Brian offering him the post. He accepted and it was great to have at my side a much younger man with fresh ideas. We worked well as a team and I was disappointed when he eventually left to take on the manager's job at Stenhousemuir.

We started the season well and started to progress in the Challenge Cup defeating Cowdenbeath and Airdrie. In the quarter-final we had to make the long midweek trip to Dingwall to play Ross County. The match went to extra time and we scraped through thanks to goals from Willie Irvine and Mark Donaghy a skilful midfielder (and now a successful football agent) I had inherited from Tom Hendrie. We defeated Stirling Albion in the semi-final and faced Inverness Caley Thistle in the final at Airdrie's Excelsior Stadium. The Alloa team that day was: Cairns

McAneny Valentine Beaton

Boyle Little Gary Clark Derek Clark

Wilson Cameron Irvine

That match was one of the best games I was ever involved in – Inverness were much better than us but could not handle Willie Irvine and Martin Cameron. At the end of 90 minutes it was 3-3 and so it went to extra-time. Both teams scored in the additional 30 minutes and now it was a penalty shoot-out. After each team had taken five penalties the score was tied at 4-4 and so it was on to "sudden death". As was always I had nominated only five penalty takers assuming a sixth would not be necessary. But wait, what was happening, my goalkeeper, Mark Cairns was striding up to take the sixth penalty. During penalty shoot-outs managers are not allowed on the pitch and so I jumped out of the dug-out and ran on to the pitch to try and stop him. Too late! He smashed the ball into the roof of the net and went back into goal and saved their sixth penalty and won the cup for us. Happy times!

On the way back to Alloa for the party, we had a singsong on the bus with son Max (who was a substitute and had played for an hour), daughter Carol and I leading the singing in best Von Trapp style. Carol was then twelve and had started to come to most of the matches and sit in the dug-out with me. Son Kevan seldom missed a match his brother played in and so my time at Alloa was quite a family affair. I was also pretty smug in that, as I had done at Stenhousemuir, I had taken Alloa to their first ever national trophy.

Just after the Challenge Cup Final I signed Andy Walker who was close to the end of a long and successful career and was without a club. I admired him greatly and was delighted when he agreed to sign.

In the Scottish Cup we were drawn against Whitehill Welfare – the second year in a row that I would facing my pal Mickey Lawson's team. As in the previous year we scraped a draw at Whitehill but this time beat them fairly comfortably at Alloa. In the third round we were drawn away to Kilmarnock who were doing well under manager Bobby Williamson. I went to watch them at Kilmarnock on a Wednesday night and took twelve year old daughter Carol with me. Ally McCoist had left Rangers and was playing for Kilmarnock – but not that night as he was injured. At half-time I said hello to him and introduced him to Carol who had juice in one hand and a pie in the other. "I cannae shake her hand Terry – is it OK if I give her a kiss" and at that he planted one on her cheek and made a wee girl happy.

I spent almost thirty years of my life preparing teams for matches but the best job I ever did was probably in that game against Kilmarnock. Son Max was designated to man-mark Ian Durrant who, although less potent than in his halcyon days with Rangers and Scotland, was still a genuinely creative player and I also played Mark Donaghy as a "false winger" (playing in off the wing) to combat their left-back who was a threat going forward. We drew 0-0 and won the replay 1-0 at Alloa thanks to a Martin Cameron goal

In the fourth round we played Dundee United at home and for about 75 minutes outplayed them and were 2-0 in the lead. Our keeper, Mark Cairns, was then quite badly injured and I had to replace him with a 17 year old from the youth team whom I had never seen playing – the finances of the club were such that we could not afford two experienced goalkeepers. The match ended 2-2 and, the following Wednesday, we went up to Tannadice for the replay with the youngster still in goal.

Prior to the match, as I was supervising the players' warm-up on the pitch, Andy Walker approached me and said that he did not want to be substituted – I had taken him off in the two matches immediately previous. I said nothing to him but was inwardly seething at his having the gall to try and pressure me in that way. The game did not go well for us (lost 4-0) and early in the second-half I decided to substitute Andy. As he came off the pitch he started to shout loudly at me in an abusive way using language that was on the north side of colourful. I said little at the time but on the following Tuesday at training I met with him in my office and informed him that he was fined two weeks wages (the maximum allowed) and that I would no longer select him for the team. Andy was taken aback and said that he had, on occasion, used stronger language to other managers. I told him that I was not "other managers". Before the last game of the season, at home to Queen of the South, Andy came to see me and asked if he could play in the game since it was going to be his last game in football as he was retiring. I agreed – we won and he scored a hat-trick!

When I look back on my treatment of Andy Walker it bothers me and I now regret the action I took and think that it was too severe. But, as I have stated, football management does force autocracy on you and, at the time, I was close to sixty, getting grumpier, and just not prepared to have players take any kind of liberty. To be successful as a manager you have to treat players well but they must operate within the strictures you set out. At the start of every season all my players were handed a short document titled "Terry's Rules" which detailed everything expected of them. The parameters of behaviour you define must be reasonable and accepted by the players but once a player acts outwith what is expected you must be prepared to take action. Two examples:

At Alloa two players are subbed, go straight into the dressing room, get changed and head off home and are not there after the match when I am making my "closing comments" to the players. At training the following Tuesday I interview both of them individually in my office, forcibly point out that their behaviour was unacceptable, and then have a meeting of all the players and stress to them that, when they are subbed, they are not allowed to "fuck off home".

At Alloa players were required to report to the ground at 1.30 pm for a 3.00 pm kick-off. One Saturday I was held up getting out of Edinburgh and arrived in the car park just before 2.00 pm, just as one of the players was getting out of his car. At training the following Tuesday I called him into my office and told him that he had arrived late on Saturday. He replied that he had got to the ground before me.

"What's that got to do with anything?"

"So you're saying that there are rules for the players and different rules for you."

"Well at least you got that fucking right! I am the manager!" A few days later he asked to be released from his contract and I agreed to do so.

When football managers are sacked you often hear, "Well, they lost the dressing room." The truth is that if players are treated with politeness and consideration it is difficult to "lose the dressing room" unless you are just not all that good a manager. Players expect a disciplined environment and will react badly to the lack of one. They expect to be able to express their views and allowing this to happen is all part of being a successful manager. The weighting that the manager puts on the opinions of the players is another thing – the manager has to make sure that he is managing the players and not the other way around. I always listened to what the players had to say and often would run over tactical ideas with individual players in order to ensure that I was asking them to do something with which they were happy. But generally the players did a lot more listening to me than I did to them. A new goalkeeper would say to me, "This is how I like the defensive wall arranged" and I would reply, "No, I decide what we do at all set plays." If a manager lets himself be led by what his players are saying that manager is in trouble. Back to Andy Walker – he is now doing great as a football reporter and is frequently on television and my conscience is a bit easier.

Just after the defeat by Dundee United I took striker Colin Nish on loan. Like Kenny Miller, Colin had been a pupil of mine at Musselburgh Grammar and was now 18 and a full-time player with Dunfermline. He played the last 13 matches in the league and formed a striking partnership with Willie Irvine and Martin Cameron that Second Division defenders could not cope with. We finished the season in second place in the league behind Clyde and were promoted to the First Division. Colin Nish had a long career and is currently playing for Cowdenbeath – he is the 10th highest ever goal scorer in the Scottish Premiership.

Soon after the end of the season Bristol Rovers, managed by Ian Holloway, bought Martin Cameron for £100,000. Colin Nish returned to Dunfermline and so I had lost both strikers – not the best preparation for the following season when I would be the only part-time manager of the only part-time team in the division. I was keen to sign Ian Harty who was doing well at Stranraer but the directors refused to pay the money required which was much less than half of what we had received for Martin Cameron. The only striker I had was 36 year old Willie Irvine and so I desperately needed to find support for him. I felt let down by the directors and at that point did think about resigning. However I really liked the people I was working for and after my tough time at school I was not in the mood for a change of club – at that time thoughts of retiring from football had not entered my head. We did pay Stenhousemuir £26,000 for Ross Hamilton who was fast, a team player but not a natural finisher and for the rest of my time at Alloa scoring goals was a problem.

In the close season Brian Fairlie, my assistant manager, left to become manager of Stenhousemuir who had departed company with my close friend Graeme Armstrong. Finding a replacement for Brian was therefore easy and Louis became my assistant manager as he had been for many years at Stenhousemuir.

Season 2000/2001 was a struggle – we went out early in all the cups, finished second bottom of the league and were relegated. It was a hard year for me and I remember telling a friend that if you were looking for a challenging life you should try running a large secondary school and at the same time manage a part-time professional football team in a league where all your opponents were full-time.

We went into the following season with a strong defence because I had added to the squad Steven Thomson from Hamilton and Greg Watson from Livingston and these two, along with Craig Valentine, gave us a powerful back-three. I also recruited young keeper Derek Soutar on loan from Dundee and he did really well. As well as the aforementioned I signed Gareth Hutchison from Falkirk, Gareth Evans from Airdrie, Keith Knox from Stranraer and Jimmy Fisher from Stenhousemuir. All four were "getting on in years" but were all good professionals and guaranteed to give of their best in every match.

The new signings did not disappoint and we started the 2001/2002 season well and did well in the Challenge Cup beating East Stirling, Inverness, Stranraer and then Clyde in the semi-final. We now faced Airdrie in the final at Clyde's Broadwood Stadium and now I get on one of my hobby horses!

Airdrie were playing in the First Division and were in administration having squandered the money they had received from the sale of their Broomfield ground. In spite of being in administration they were allowed to sign players – something that angered me greatly. Owen Coyle was playing for Ross County and I heard that they were prepared to release him from his contract. I phoned him and made him what for Alloa was a generous offer. Owen, a great lad, thanked me for my interest and said that he would consider it. A short time later he signed for in-administration and "up to their eyes in debt" Airdrie. That would not be allowed today but back then the football authorities were terrified of clubs going out of business and were bending the rules to try and prevent that happening – fairness became a secondary consideration.

Airdrie, managed by Ian McCall, won 2-1 and, to rub salt into my wounds, Owen Coyle scored one of their goals. At the end of the season Airdrie resigned from the Scottish Football League and went into liquidation.

They returned the following season as Airdrie United. The Alloa team that day was:

Soutar

Thomson   Valentine   Watson

Knox   Little   Fisher   Seaton

Walker   Hamilton   Hutchison

Subs: Curran, Evans, Irvine, Christie, McQueen.

Before the match I had to decide whether or not to play Willie Irvine who was a couple of months away from his 38th birthday. I felt that age was at last catching up with Willie and decided not to play him. He was upset and I felt bad about making him unhappy but I had to pick what I thought was our best team – I still wonder if I should have played him.

That season we were drawn against Celtic in the third round of the Scottish Cup. This was the only time I faced Celtic as a manager and it I was a game I like to forget. Because of worries about the size of the crowd the match was played at Falkirk. Celtic were going strong under Martin O'Neil and thumped us 5-0 with the difference in quality obvious to all.

We finished second in the league and were once again promoted to the First Division and again I knew I faced a massive challenge in trying to keep us in the higher division.

As always I was on the look out for an older player who would give us a bit of quality and I found just the man in 35 year old mid-fielder Derek Ferguson who, at the end of the season, had quit as player-manager of Clydebank. Derek had won two Scottish caps and had played for Rangers, Hearts, Sunderland, Falkirk and Dunfermline. He took a little time to come to terms with having a schoolteacher as manager but, in the latter part of the season, he was the best midfielder in the league; it was a pleasure watching him. We did much better than we had two years previously but we did find it hard, and, on the last day of the season, were in second bottom position with the same points as Ross County who had a better goal difference. We hammered St Mirren but unfortunately they beat Ayr United comfortably and we were relegated on goal difference.

It was a huge blow to everyone at the club and I could see the enthusiasm draining out of the board of directors. Money became much tighter and for the second time I had to persuade my wife Susan that a small portion of our income should go as a contribution to a player I wanted to sign. Although the only sizeable transfer fee the club had paid out was the £26,000 to Stenhousemuir for Ross Hamilton, they were paying much higher salaries than ever before as I persuaded them of the need to do so to attract decent players. Their enthusiasm for continuing this level of expenditure was wearing thin and, in order to clinch the signing of a particular player I wanted, I dipped into my own pocket and contributed a small amount to his wages that was sufficient to close the deal. At the time

Alloa were paying me the £12,000 a year which was the most I had ever been paid and, when you added this to my headteacher earnings, I was comfortably off although far from rich. But what did a few bob matter if it improved the team!

I lost several players (including Derek Ferguson) who were out of contract and we started the 2003/2004 season with the poorest squad I had managed for years. My 61st birthday was not far away and, although I had retired from teaching and should have had more energy for football, I was exhausted; driving to Alloa for training was becoming a problem for me. Early in November we were defeated at home by Berwick Rangers. Immediately after the match I informed the secretary, Ewen Cameron, that I was resigning. That night I went to a schools' football dinner in Glasgow feeling terrible. I was sad at leaving the game I loved and that had been so big a part of my life but I could not face once again having a poor team and struggling to make them better.

I had done two jobs for 43 years and needed a rest. As always when I was stressed my eczema was playing up and I knew that if I did not slow down I was going to make myself ill. Looking back I take pride in that all the clubs I managed improved under my management and that, with my three small part-time clubs, the only teams that I did not defeat were Hearts, Rangers and Celtic although I did draw with Rangers and took Hearts to a penalty shoot-out. Often I am asked how I think I would have fared if I had gone in to full-time football management. We will never know, but football is football and I think I might have done alright.

On Not Becoming Hibs' Manager and Falling Out with Referees

I was brought up a Hibs' fan and attended my first match when about four. In our family our happiness was directly proportional to the fortunes of the Hibernian Football Club. I could have signed for Hibs as a youngster but I did not think I would be good enough to be a Hibs player and preferred to try my luck at distant Dundee. I never thought about being manager of the club I loved until I started to do well as Meadowbank Thistle manager and then I started to dream.

In 1986 John Blackley was sacked as manager by chairman Kenny Waugh and I received a phone call asking me to come for an interview at the house of Gregor Cowan, who at the time was a director of the club. Gregor lived in the Trinity area of Edinburgh and I remember driving to the meeting nervous but excited.

The meeting went well and I left with the clear impression that I was about to be the new manager of Hibs. Kenny Waugh never uttered the words, "Terry the job is yours" but his words were only marginally less definitive. The next night Hibs were playing away to Clydebank and I went to the match with Susan, Kevan, Max and Mickey Lawson (who was to be my assistant manager) to run the eye over my new charges.

The next day Stewart Brown had a story in the Edinburgh Evening News stating that Terry Christie was to be the next Hibs' manager. I could not get the smile of my face and then a couple of days went by and I heard no more from Kenny Waugh and started to worry.

Stewart Brown phoned me using the type of voice normally used to tell someone that a member of the family has passed away. He broke the news that Alex Miller was to be appointed and not me. Seemingly Alex's assistant manager, Peter Cormack, had phoned Kenny Waugh to let him know that Alex, then manager of St Mirren, would be interested in the Easter Road job. Alex was appointed and I heard no more from anybody associated with Hibs.

I was hugely disappointed but picked myself up and got on with running Ainslie Park High School and Meadowbank Thistle – but I still had a dream.

One Sunday morning in 1991 I was having a long lie (Susan and Carol were at her parents' house in Wilmslow) when the phone rang and I found myself speaking to Tom Farmer, the owner of both Kwik Fit and Hibs who were not doing too well. He asked me to meet him in the Caledonian Hotel at the west end of Princes Street. The interview went well and again, although, he never said, "Looking forward to having you as manager, Terry" I left the interview thinking that the job was mine. Tom told me that a close friend of his, Allan Munro, would be in touch with me in a few days. I did speak to Allan but it was 15 years later at Duddingston Golf Club. Nobody from Hibs got in touch and Alex Miller continued as manager and the fortunes of the team picked up. But I still kept dreaming!

We now move on to 1996 when Hibs and Alex Miller parted company. Dougie Cromb was chairman of Hibs and Tom O'Malley, a friend of mine, was a director. I had known Tom for many years dating back to when we were both pupils at Holy Cross Academy. He was headteacher at St David's High School, Dalkeith, and he had helped me get my first job in teaching. Tom phoned me and asked me to come and see him in his North Berwick home. When I spoke to him he was keen that I become Hibs manager and during our meeting he called Hibs owner, Tom Farmer, and reported to me that Tom was equally enthusiastic about my appointment. I left North Berwick walking tall – surely I was not about to be a three-time loser. The days passed without my hearing anything and "déjà vu" started to kick in. Inevitably I received a call from Tom saying that Jim Duffy was to be the new manager. He told me that Dougie Cromb had opposed my appointment and threatened to resign if I became manager. I can't think of anything I did to upset Dougie but, there it was, and I stopped dreaming.

When I was a player I seldom got into trouble with referees. I hardly ever committed a foul and the only time I was sent off my appeal was upheld. When I became a manager, and particularly when I started to manage a professional team, I began to view referees in a different light.

Let me make it clear, I like and respect referees and many of them are good friends of mine and a few are close friends. Most referees go into it because they were not good enough as players and refereeing was a way to stay involved in the game they loved. The problem with refereeing is that it is so difficult. To be a good referee you have to be fit, decisive, a good people manager, calm under pressure and have just about all the qualities required of an officer in the SAS. The reason that there are so few wonderful referees are that referees are human and most of them at some time are let down by their human frailties.

Referees hate to be accused of favouring one team over another but they do; they favour the home team over the away team and they favour the big club over the small club. They try not to do this but they are human and they cannot help themselves. The power of peer pressure means that they are loath to disappoint the majority of spectators at the match who are normally associated with the home team or the bigger club. That does not make them bad people it only emphasises their humanity.

When I became manager of Meadowbank Thistle I soon realised that, as the new kid on the block with very few fans, we were not getting a fair break with referees. I had to find a way of exerting more peer pressure on them, but how? My answer was to act as if I was the manager of a big club and to make enough noise myself so as to compensate for the lack of actual fans. I also studied the "Laws of the Game" so that my knowledge of the rules was at least equal to (and often greater) than that of the referee. There in nothing that unsettles a referee more than being told that they have made a mistake with regard to the Laws of the Game.

I was careful not to shout continually because then you become background noise. I reserved my shouting for when I thought the referee had made an error. I taught my players not to foul because I hate fouling and moreover the subsequent free kick allows the opposition to deliver a dangerous ball into your penalty area. Many managers actively encourage their players to foul and so I reserved most of my comments to the referee when I felt he had not awarded a free kick to us. I never complained when he gave a free kick against us – to do so would have made me just another manager who wanted his players to be allowed to kick the other team. I made a note of the free kicks awarded against individual opposition players and would shout out things like, "That's his fourth foul ref.". The manager in the other dug-out would scream, "Are you fucking trying to get my players booked?" and I would reply, "No, I am trying to get the referee to stop them kicking my players."

All of this worked and we started to get much more of a fair shake from referees. I knew that the referee who was allocated a Meadowbank game received the sympathy of his colleagues before the match. "Good luck, you will have that wee pest Christie to put up with."

But occasionally I did overstep the mark. I was sent to the stand on six occasions but, you will be surprised to hear, that I was to blame only once – the other five times the referees reacted badly to my pointing out the error of their ways.

The time I was to blame was early in my career at Meadowbank when I complained to the referee too often and too loudly about trivial matters. He got fed up of me and rightly sent me to the stand. I appeared before the "powers that be" and was banned from the touchline for a month.

But I was to become an even bigger pest! Meadowbank Stadium has only one stand and during matches all the fans were easily accommodated in it. Across from the main stand is some terracing on top of which is a walkway. When I became manager of Meadowbank Thistle I noticed that some players would perform less well when they were playing on the opposite side of the pitch away from the main stand. I therefore had our dugout changed from in front of the stand over to the other side so that I could address the problem of distant players losing interest. The opposition dugout stayed where it was and this had the advantage that my staff and myself could not get involved with the staff of the opposition. Or, to put it another way, I would not be able to hear the abuse being shouted at me.

During my ban I decided not to sit in the stand but instead to use the walkway opposite the main stand. The advantage of this was that I could move up and down the pitch with the play and, even better, could stand directly behind the linesman, and shout at him to put his flag up for offside and sometimes scold him when he failed to do so. I enjoyed doing this so much that I stayed on the walkway for the rest of my time as manager of Meadowbank.

The second time I was sent from the pitch the referee was Jim McCluskey, one of the nicest people you could meet. It was late in a match against Airdrie at Broomfield when Graeme Armstrong, in those days a flying left winger, was tripped in the opponents penalty box with seconds to go and the score 1-1. Jim gave a corner and not a penalty and I went ballistic. The linesman called him over and he sent me to the stand. Afterwards in the tea-room I was chatting to the Airdrie manager, Gordon McQueen (best headed goal ever at Wembley for Scotland in 1977), when referee Jim came in for a cuppa. To my great pleasure Gordon said, "What about you no giving a penalty and sending Terry to the stand Jim – it was a stonewaller." I was fined and banned from the dugout.

Number three was the funniest. Meadowbank were playing Partick Thistle at Firhill when, a few seconds into the game, their Colin McGlashan made a forward run. The nearside linesman snapped up his flag indicating that Colin was offside. Referee Brian McGinley waved down the flag and Colin went through and stuck the ball in the net for a goal. I jumped out the dugout and started to shout at Brian that he should have given an offside decision. He ran across to me and said, "Terry I've made an arse of it but I am not changing my mind. Get back in your dugout." I went back to the dugout an angry man and threw the pen I was holding into the dugout. Now the dugouts at Firhill are made of Perspex and have a rounded hood and when the pen hit the rounded Perspex roof it made a noise not unlike a machine gun. The linesman (Wee John from Linlithgow) called Brian over who sent me to the stand. The game was less than two minutes old. Getting to the stand was not easy because the changing rooms at Firhill are detached from the main stand and so I had to go into the changing rooms and from there out into the street at the back of the stand. When I got out into the street the fans were still coming in and a Partick Thistle fan on seeing me said, "Cannae be much of a game, Terry." But then it got worse – the commissioner on the main door had been called away and it was several minutes before he could be found and give permission for me to take a seat in the stand where, on my entrance, I was roundly booed by all the Partick fans. Happy ending however – we won the match. At the hearing in the SFA's headquarters in Park Gardens, Glasgow, Brian McGinlay was called to give evidence. To my amazement he admitted making an error and I got off and my respect for Scotland's best ever referee took a quantum leap.

The fourth time was in midwinter at Ayr with Gerry Evans refereeing. Gerry did not drive but took the bus or train to all his matches such was his love for the game. When not refereeing his full-time job was looking after some of Scotland's most challenging young people.

All in all a bit of a saint and you had to try hard to get on his wrong side – but I managed to do it. When I arrived at Somerset and went onto the pitch I could not believe that the match was to be played. Most of the surface was fine but there was a strip some 15 yards wide, hidden from the sun by the grandstand that was covered in white frost and bone hard. I went to see Gerry and told him as forcibly as was possible that the game should not be played. He listened to me and then said that it was to go ahead. Early on he slipped and fell heavily but still he continued with the match. It was the winter of 1995 when I had a good Stenhousemuir side one of the stars of which was Gareth Hutchison. After about 30 minutes Gareth slipped and fell heavily. That was too much for me. I ran on to the pitch and started to jump up and down shouting at Gerry that it was dangerous. Imagine a toddler in a temper in a supermarket jumping up and down – well that will give you an accurate picture of how headteacher Christie was behaving. I was sent to the stand, fined and banned and, by the way, we lost.

I was hard done by the fifth time. Stenhousemuir were playing Livingston and their centre-half, Grant Tierney, who had captained Meadowbank Thistle, kept fouling our centre-forward Paul Hunter. In the first-half the referee, John Rowbottom gave eight fouls against Grant but never booked him. I knew it was eight because I made a note each time he fouled Paul. Coming off the pitch at half-time I confronted the referee and told him that Grant had fouled Paul eight times and he had done nothing about it. He told me to get on my way. As I entered our changing room I turned and said to him, "You are the referee and it is your job to implement the laws of the game." Shortly afterwards there was a knock on the changing room door – it was one of the linesmen who politely told me that Mr Rowbottom wished to see me in his changing room. I went along to the referee's room and John told me that he was reporting me to the SFA because of the remarks I had made. After the match (defeat) I was not too worried thinking that I could not be punished for making a remark of a factual nature. At the hearing John gave evidence and when asked what I had said he told those present that I uttered the words, "You are the referee and it is your job to implement the laws of the game." When I heard his accurate account of what I had said I breathed a sigh of relief thinking "they surely cannot punish me for correctly defining the function of the referee". I was fined and given a lengthy ban and I think the words "serial offender" were used to describe me.

Now the sixth time I was unlucky. In 2002 the laws of the game were changed so that an injured player who received treatment on the pitch had to leave the pitch after receiving treatment. All managers were called to SFA headquarters, now at Hampden Park, and the change was explained to us with great emphasis being placed on its mandatory nature. Third game of the season and Alloa are playing Morton at Greenock. Their player is injured and, after receiving treatment, is allowed to stay on the pitch. I complain loudly that he should have left the pitch and the referee, Ian Fyfe, sends me to the stand. At the hearing I eloquently explained that I was only upholding the new mandatory law. I was listened to with some sympathy and understanding and was then fined and banned from the dugout.

In my time in football the best referee was Brian McGinley with Hugh Dallas a close second. Two other referees I admired were George Smith and Willie Young who were both outstanding in the way they managed the players. Willie is a lawyer by trade and a talented after dinner speaker. We had a disagreement during a midweek match at Alloa where Willie was a wee bit short of his usual high standard. Our defender Craig Valentine was fouled deep in our own half but managed to retain possession of the ball and so Willie did not give a free-kick but waved for play to continue. "Vally" was the type of player who is at his best when the opposition have the ball and so when Willie let play continue I feared the worst. Sure enough, Vally's pass was intercepted by an opponent who smashed the ball into our net. I started to shout at Willie who came running over to me. "Terry, you cannot shout at me like that even if I did make a mistake." I continued to rant. "Terry, if you don't stop I am going to have to send you to the stand." "Well at least that will get me further away from you Willie." He turned and ran back on to the pitch shaking his head.

Refereeing is difficult – I should know because I did it with my school teams most Saturday mornings for 30 years but that did not stop me from behaving like a wee arse on Saturday afternoons.

Life in the Slow Lane

I retired from teaching in August 2003 and from football the following November and now looked forward to a rest. As you get older people you love leave you and so it was with me. The best motivation a person can have is to be loved by someone who is proud of you and who expects high standards from you in everything you do. For me that person was my mother, Wee Bridget. In 1997 she was diagnosed with cervical cancer and received radiation treatment. Five years later the cancer returned and quickly she became ill. I remember having to help her into the bath and her saying to me "Don't look." To which I replied, "Ma, don't worry, there's no chance I am going to look at you." As she got older, during the Easter school holidays, I used to take her and my daughter, Carol, to Ireland to see all her friends and relatives in Arigna and will never forget the three of us squeezing into the only bed available in a pub in Drumshambo – Carol was in the middle. I saw her three or four times a week but this was never enough for her and she was always at me to visit her. With the school and football this was not easy and I was nearing sixty and was knackered; but I did my best. "Ma, I will come for half-an-hour after school before I go to Alloa but you are not allowed to talk." "OK, son I will not ask any questions, I will keep quiet." Of course when I got there she bombarded me with questions. I would be trying to have a nap on her couch and she would be sitting beside me watching me. "Ma, fuck off I am trying to get a nap." "Sorry son, but go and tell me something." "What do you want me to tell you?" "Anything " was her normal reply.

I will never forget her last words to me. I was sitting at her bedside in hospital with Margaret (my first wife) when Bridget regained consciousness and saw that I was crying, "Don't get down", were the last words she spoke to me. I was heartbroken – I had been a "mummy's boy" all my life and now she was gone. That was 13 years ago and I still miss her dreadfully.

Less than a year later I was again grieving. Murray McDermott was my goalkeeper in the Meadowbank Thistle team that won the Second Division in 1987 and had been one of my closest friends for many years. Murray was handsome, bright, good-natured fit as a fiddle and just someone you never thought could become ill; but he did. He was diagnosed with pancreatic cancer and died at age 53. Susan and I see his lovely wife, Catrina, on most Saturday nights and try not to talk about how much we miss Murray.

On a brighter note I now had no work to go to and could enjoy myself. I had spent 37 years teaching in comprehensive schools that were challenging and had sometimes wondered what it would be like to teach in the private sector where behaviour was much less of an issue. The mother of one of my teachers at Musselburgh Grammar was depute head at George Watson's and I asked her daughter to speak to her mother and see if it could be arranged for me to spend one day teaching in the private sector. And so it was that one Monday I turned up at George Watson's as a supply teacher. Being a left wing liberal and a member of the Labour Party I just knew I was going to hate it – and of course I loved it! The kids were great, although it was a bit off putting when I walked into the first class I was taking and a girl called out, "Sir, are you a football manager?" I will always be a strong believer in state education but that does not prevent me recognising that many wonderful children attend private schools.

After a few months rest I needed something to do (besides golfing and playing chess on the computer) and so I went back to work for East Lothian Council as a supply teacher and spent a few months teaching mathematics and chemistry part-time at Knox Academy in Haddington and Ross High School in Tranent. I enjoyed it but it was hard work and enforcing discipline was just that little bit more difficult when you are not the headteacher!

I then successfully applied for the post of General Manager at Duddingston Golf Club where I had been a member for many years. The job involved not only looking after the golf side of things but also managing the bar and restaurant and I was therefore on a sharp learning curve. If you have managed to read as far as this you will have realised that I have a good conceit of myself. I have to admit, however, to being less than a great success as manager of Duddingston Golf Club. I was well into my sixties and found it difficult to cope with the committee structure and the demands of some of the members. One day I was working in my office when the door was thrown open and an irate member was standing there with a bread roll in his hand. "What do you think of this?" he asked showing me the roll. "Looks like a sausage roll to me", I replied. "Sausage roll, sausage roll - it's got only two sausages on it!" After three years in the job, and working some 55 hours a week, I retired at age 67 determined never again to work but to try and enjoy life. And then my brother Peter became ill.

Although he was a "Leither" Peter lived in Tranent, the home of his late partner, Pat. Every morning he would get the bus from Tranent into Edinburgh to shoplift and then spend the rest of the day drinking with his pals in one of Leith's many pubs. I met with him regularly, as I had done all my life. He had two children Peter and Angela. Peter had moved to London and Angela was the centre of my brother's universe. They were as close as any father and daughter could be and Peter thought the world of her. Just after I had finished working at Duddingston Golf Club he was diagnosed with rectal cancer and underwent surgery followed by chemotherapy. Angela worked full-time and so during the week I looked after him and saw him every day except Sundays. After battling for a couple of years he became very ill and could get about only by using a wheelchair. I was the wheelchair driver and Peter would regularly give me feedback on my performance with comments such as, "You're fucking hopeless at driving a wheelchair." He never complained about his illness but he was as cantankerous as he had always been and shopping with him was a nightmare because ill health had not reduced his enthusiasm for stealing. I was one day pushing him round the supermarket when he said, "Take me to the carrots." I did as instructed. "Get me closer." I pushed him closer and he stretched out, picked up a carrot, and put it in his pocket and said to me, "Shut you're fucking mouth." I did as instructed and, I am ashamed to say, became an accomplice in the theft of a carrot.

Peter last spoke to me the day before he died. Angela and I were at his bedside when he awoke from his sleep and said, "Where's Terry?" I said, "I am here." "Hold my hands." I held his hands. "Now pull me up. I am getting up." "No Peter, you cannae get up, you're to have a day in bed." "Are you telling me I cannae get up?" "That's right." He then spoke to me for the last time, "Well, you can go and fuck off!" He never regained consciousness after that and passed away the next day.

I was heartbroken. What I felt for Peter was more than love. He had bullied me, embarrassed me, but, he was my brother and was part of my being, and helping and caring for him was as natural as looking after myself.

There is one important part of my life about which I have said little – parenthood. I have three children: Kevan (18 September 1968); Max (7 November 1971) and Carol (20 March 1987). When discussions about parenthood come up I always say, "Well, I never gave it a thought – I just did what came naturally to me." And this is true and I am lucky to have three wonderful kids all of whom have distinct personalities and all of whom, in their own way, are "characters".

This "never gave it a thought" approach did sometimes go awry:

- Kevan was nine and was playing football for Portobello Thistle. Since he could walk I had him kicking a ball and I was overjoyed that he had a real talent. "My son is going to be a player" was often my last thought before falling asleep. He played his first match for Portobello Thistle and slowly I had to accept the obvious – he could control the ball but could not run. I broke the news to him gently, "Son, you have got great skill but you cannae run. You will have to think of a career other than professional football." For a nine year old he took the news well but I was disappointed that he felt he had to mention the incident in his best man's speech when his brother married Lisa.

- Max was a handful as a child – loveable but naughty. At age 10 he had found a new game – playing in his dad's car and leaving it with the doors locked and the keys inside the car. He did this for the umpteenth time one Sunday morning and I lost my head. I chased him but, unlike Kev, he could run, and I was having difficulty catching him so as to administer the heavy hand he deserved. Instinct took over and I tripped him and he fell heavily and burst out crying. The wind had been knocked out of him and his knee was bleeding. I felt bad and started to feel even worse when I realised that in one hour's time he was due to play for Portobello Thistle at the Inch. "I am no playing, and I am going to tell everybody what you did to me." He went on to the pitch limping badly and giving his dad the "evils" but to my relief did not "shop" me to the men who ran the team.

- Carol never misbehaved and is the daughter every father would like to have – I adore her. Fortunately she has recovered well from the information I gave her when she was six. My mind must have been on Saturday's game when she asked me where babies came from and I told her the truth. A little while later I must have been again distracted when I uttered the words, "Of course there's no Santa." Her tears made me feel terrible but I gave her a fruit scone and jam and she cheered up.

Kev is a journalist with "The Scotsman", Max is a financial adviser and has a company called "Clarity" (0131 661 2777) where he works closely with his stepmum, Sue, and Carol is a secondary school modern languages teacher. Kev is married to Margo, Max to Lisa and Carol lives with her fiance Alex. I have five terrific grandchildren, Jack, Ellie, Charlie, Cormac and baby Terry and I no longer have any involvement in football having just retired after eight years as a match delegate at Premiership games.

Life is now about baby-sitting, football (on the telly or watching Broxburn Athletic who are managed by Max), golf, chess, reading, going out with friends, and having holidays in Spain and the United States with my darling Susan. I am having a great time!

Being full-time in teaching and part-time in football allowed me to pursue both my passions. But what would have happened if I had become manager of Hibs?

Printed in Great Britain
by Amazon